The Rock Art of Utah

FRONTISPIECE Barrier Canyon Style painting, the Bird Site, Horse Canyon. Photograph by Dean Brimhall.

The Rock Art of Utah

A STUDY FROM THE

DONALD SCOTT COLLECTION

Polly Schaafsma

University of Utah Press
Salt Lake City

Cover photograph: Fremont figure with antlers and long earrings, Moab.

2004 2003

5 4

Library of Congress Cataloging-in-Publication Data

Schaafsma, Polly.
    The rock art of Utah : a study from the Donald Scott Collection / Polly Schaafsma.
      p. cm.
    Originally published: Cambridge : Peabody Museum of Archaeology and Ethnology, Harvard University, 1971, in series: Papers of the Peabody Museum of Archaeology and Ethnology ; vol. 65.
    Includes bibliographical references.
    ISBN 0-87480-435-3 (alk. paper)
    1. Indians of North America—Utah—Antiquities. 2. Rock paintings—Utah. 3. Petroglyphs—Utah. 4. Utah—Antiquities.
I. Scott, Donald, 1879–1967. II. Title.
E78.U55S33 1994
709'.01'1309792—dc20   93-2052

Contents

Plates

Figures

Tables

Preface

(1994)

On a rainy New England day in November 1968, accompanied by Mrs. Iris Thomas and Louise Scott, I was led to a dark, narrow corner room in the Peabody Museum where the Donald Scott rock art files resided under lock and key. I would spend a couple of days there examining sketchy field notes, photos, and drawings of rock paintings and petroglyphs from all over North America to decide what material I needed to make a book. As mentioned by J. O. Brew in the note following this preface, I discovered that the Utah drawers were the focus of the collection. This is where Mr. Scott began his collection in 1928, and this large body of photographs seemed to hold the most promise for study.

In the late sixties, when rock art was just beginning to find a place within the archaeological discipline, this collection of photos and drawings of petroglyphs and paintings from the remote canyon walls of Utah was a most unusual assemblage of data. Some of it represented a rather extensive documentation of specific sites by individuals like Reagan and Nusbaum, but in most cases material had been collected by members of the Claflin-Emerson Expedition, Frank Beckwith, Louis Schellbach and others as opportunity permitted.

Further appraisal of the material at a later date led to the decision to omit the San Juan region of southeastern Utah from the volume. It was not as well covered by the files, and culturally it belonged with the Anasazi more appropriately connected with prehistoric northern Arizona and New Mexico—another subject in itself. In retrospect it is regrettable that Basketmaker rock art was not included in this study. Rock art of the San Juan Basketmakers is an integral part of the "Utah Tradition" that features the large anthropomorphic figures of the Barrier Canyon and Fremont styles and styles linked as well by apparent cultural and ideological relationships. As it was, however, a short section on the San Juan figures was included for comparative purposes (pp. 139-41). Basketmaker rock art has subsequently been described elsewhere (Schaafsma 1980:108–19; and Cole 1989).

The strength of the Scott Files lay in the Fremont area to the north and in records of the Great Basin and Virgin-Kayenta rock art in the west. Here I was able to discover patterns that resulted in the definition of several Utah rock art styles. Next an attempt was made to associate these styles with various archaeological components, largely the Archaic and Fremont regional divisions. This initial ordering of the rock art material was viewed as a base for future research. Thus the resulting volume is descriptive in character, with a focus on the formal aspects of elements and style. Aspects of chronology are a major concern, as is the evidence for cultural relationships beyond the regions discussed. What the content of this rock art signified and how it functioned for its creators are topics only briefly considered. This lack was partly the result of restrictions imposed by the nature of the study itself—one conducted strictly on photos and drawings. As a result, the site contexts were missing, the scale of the figures was usually unknown, the available data for any given site was usually only partial, and so forth.

Also I would like to note that in many of the photographs taken early in the twentieth century, including those by Reagan and Nusbaum and Beckwith, the rock art was chalked to enhance its clarity. This is a destructive practice, no longer condoned. Chalking usually results in the misrepresentation of the original rock art imagery and is highly detrimental to the preservation and integrity of petroglyphs and rock paintings.

When the University of Utah Press decided to republish this volume, twenty-three years later, it was decided not to rewrite the book in an effort to catch up with intervening studies. This edition, however, is embellished with some new photographs, and in addition I will take this opportunity to make some summary comments on subsequent research developments in Utah rock art.

Two decades later, many more sites have been discovered and documented. Following the original publication of this volume and a brief statewide field survey arranged by Jesse Jennings to complete field data on the well-known sites (Schaafsma 1970), a broad field survey in the late 1970s by Kenneth Castleton located and recorded many others. This work resulted in two volumes on Utah rock art that included southeastern Utah as well (Castleton 1978; 1979). Castleton with David B. Madsen later published a paper on the distribution of rock art elements and styles (Castleton and Madsen 1981). In addition, localities that have received notable attention in terms of site documentation and analysis are those in National Park Service Canyonlands complex of southeastern Utah (Noxon and Marcus 1982; 1985; Tipps and Hewitt 1989), Nine Mile Canyon (Hurst and Louthan 1979), and Dinosaur National Park (Burton 1971). A recent synthesis by Cole (1990) of the rock art of the Colorado Plateau and Four Corners region encompasses eastern Utah.

With this enlarged data base, we know more today about the styles described herein and can add others to the roster of Utah's prehistoric art and cultural heritage. Cole in particular has defined additional style complexes for eastern Utah. The Interior Line Style, with a focus in western Wyoming, the northwestern Plains culture area, is now known to occur down the Green River drainage to east-central Utah (Cole 1990: map 6). Cole also isolates an Abajo–La Sal style north of the southeast Utah Anasazi region, as well as three periods of historic Ute rock art in eastern Utah (1990:225-51). The so-called Faces Motif, (see plate 27, this volume) has been singled out and named as a distinctive localized style in the rock art of Canyonlands. Here a number of panels of these Fremont-like anthropomorphic images have been documented, often in association with Anasazi structures and ceramics (Cole 1990:166–71; Noxon and Marcus 1985; Tipps and Hewitt 1989:113–14). Although the cultural association of this style remains in the realm of debate, recent dating of Fremont rock art in southeastern Utah (Geib and Fairley 1992; Coulam 1992) argues for a late Fremont origin.

Data on the pre-Fremont or Archaic rock art styles described in this volume have now been amplified to a considerable degree. The Glen Canyon Linear style (originally Glen Canyon Style 5 [Turner 1963:37–38]; pp. 62–65, this volume) is noted in Canyonlands National Park (Hogan et al. 1975; Tipps and Hewitt 1989:109–10). Polychrome abstract rock paintings (see pp. 61–62, this volume) are known from more sites in south-central and east-central Utah (Cole 1990:45–46; Noxon and Marcus 1985). Of major importance to this discussion is the much larger number of known Barrier Canyon sites and the great increase in their distribution, stretching along the Colorado drainage from northwestern Colorado to the Escalante in south-central Utah. In addition, a closely related style occurs in southwestern Utah (see figure 116, this volume, labeled Basketmaker following Judd 1926) and the adjacent Grand Canyon region (Allen 1992; Schaafsma 1990).

Burton (1971) proposed a chronological development for typological changes observable in Fremont Classic Vernal style pecked anthropomorphs in northeastern Utah. This chronology from fully defined figures (early) to abstracted or abbreviated ren-

ditions (late; see plate 10, upper left, this volume) is postulated on the basis of superimpositions and the use of factor analysis. Though it poses some questions, as the same variation appears in San Juan Basketmaker sites in and near Butler Wash.

Some strides have been made in the difficult realm of chronology. Revised dates have been proposed by Turner (1971) for the Glen Canyon Linear style (Style 5), pushing it significantly further back in time. Unbaked clay figurines from Cowboy Cave and Sudden Shelter typologically are like the painted anthropomorphs in the Barrier Canyon style, and some are also similarly decorated. The associated dates from 4000 B.C., or in one case 6000 B.C. (Hull and White 1980:122–25) opens the possibility of much older beginnings for the Barrier Canyon style paintings, perhaps as far back as 5000 B.C. (Schaafsma 1986:225). In another instance, excavation in a shelter where an association between a midden and a Barrier Canyon style painting seemed likely yielded a date in the vicinity of 1390 B.C. (Tipps and Hewitt 1989:125). Radiocarbon dating of an artifact from a Fremont rock art site, as well as charcoal pigment from a rock painting of a Fremont anthropomorph, produced dates more or less within the realm of expectations for the Fremont time frame, although pushing the outer limits for the Fremont culture itself (Geib and Fairley 1992). These results have interesting implications for the observable continuity between the Basketmaker–Fremont and the Faces motifs associated with Anasazi structures (Geib and Fairley 1992:164–66).

As time goes on, one would expect the application and improvement of absolute dating techniques to give us a great deal more chronometric control in this field (Bard et al. 1978; Russ et al. 1990; Whitley and Dorn 1988). This control, once achieved, will require adjustments in our thinking and how we piece together the prehistoric picture. Chronometric control is especially important for these Utah sites in which the archaeologist is faced with a long and complex rock art tradition that has often produced a confusing array of images.

Today the subject of interpretation is also a matter of increasing interest. Meaning was a secondary concern, approached with a fair degree of caution in 1971, when the preoccupation was with identifying order in the chaos of Utah rock art. Since then, scholars, including myself, have commented on and explored the shamanic implications of the Barrier Canyon style and Fremont figures (Cole 1990:77; Hedges 1985:90-92; Schaafsma 1980:71–72, 179–81; 1986:226; 1990). Furthermore, it might be added that there is now substantial evidence from the San Juan Basketmaker region to indicate that the apparent fetish heads in the hands of the imposing Classic Vernal style figures (figures 4–6 and plate 1) are in fact just that scalps that include the face (Cole 1989; 1990: figures 45, 48; Kidder and Guernsey 1919: plate 87). In the Southwest, such trophies or fetishes have rain-bringing functions in connection with corn cultivation (Schaafsma 1992).

At this writing, the ideological history of prehistoric Utah suggested by rock art might be briefly reconstructed as follows: the rock art prevailing in western Utah, characterized by abstract designs, suggests that ideological ties with the Great Basin peoples to the west prevailed for several thousand years. This continuity was broken only by rock art dominated by the presence of the Fremont anthropomorph for a limited period. In the east, the Utah Tradition of rock art, in which shamanic anthropomorphic figures predominated across a number of stylistic boundaries, suggests an on-going, powerful ideological theme embraced by the majority of eastern Utah's prehistoric people for several thousand years. Carried on into the late prehistoric period by the Fremont culture, it appears to have ended with the disappearance or waning of the Fremont between A.D. 1000 and 1300, depending on the area. Just as this visual tradition draws to a close, changes in other artifacts such as baskets, pottery, and projectile points (Adovaslo 1986:205; Fowler and Fowler 1981:145-46, 148, 153; Madsen 1986:214) indicate a major cultural break with the past. It is suggested that the cultural demise of the Fremont as well as the Virgin-Kayenta Anasazi was possibly instigated by a Numic expansion from the west, which absorbed or otherwise "destroyed" the Fremont culture (Fowler and Fowler 1981). In the Green River drainage of eastern Utah, the presence of a relatively late distinctive, rather elegant, deer or elk, with small head and long antlers (see plate 15) may have been made by Numic speaking latecomers.

I would like to take this opportunity to thank Phil Geib for his communications keeping me up to date with advances in chronology, Sally Cole for over a decade of conversations and information exchange, and especially Jeff Grathwohl of the University of Utah Press for initiating and seeing through to completion the reissuing of *The Rock Art of Utah*.

Polly Schaafsma

Acknowledgments

This monograph is the culmination of the efforts of a large number of people over a period of many years. The photographs and field notes which provided the basic data for this report are part of a large collection assembled by the late Donald Scott, Director of the Peabody Museum at Harvard University. This collection of photographs, which includes rock art from all over the world, was accumulated throughout Mr. Scott's academic career. Much of the material from the canyons of eastern Utah was obtained by Donald Scott himself and by the Claflin-Emerson archaeological reconnaissance of the area in the years between 1927 and 1931. Large numbers of photographs of Utah sites were also contributed to the files by Albert B. Reagan and Jesse Nusbaum, who worked in eastern Utah, and Frank Beckwith of Delta and Julian Steward, who recorded sites all over the central part of the state. Other investigators also made contributions to that part of the Scott collection currently under consideration. Among them were M. R. Harrington and Louis Schellbach, who photographed sites in eastern Nevada, and A. V. Kidder, Charles B. Boogher, Lewis B. Jones, and C. Sharp, who recorded various eastern Utah sites. Recent Utah contributions have been made by Dr. David DeHarport, Dr. David S. Dibble, Dean Brimhall, and Dr. David Breternitz.

Study of the Utah collection was initiated in 1968. This research was made possible through a grant provided by the Scott family. Arrangements for the use of facilities at the University of New Mexico were made through the assistance of Dr. Jack Campbell; and Dr. George Ewing of the Museum of New Mexico kindly extended the use of the library and other facilities in Santa Fe.

I would like to express my gratitude at this time to Mrs. Louise Scott, wife of the late Donald Scott, and to Dr. Donald Scott, Jr., who made this project possible and who maintained a keen and helpful interest throughout the preparation of this report. I am highly indebted to Noel Morss for his unfailing enthusiasm, extensive comments, and careful reading and editing of the manuscript throughout its development. Constructive recommendations were also contributed by Dr. James H. Gunnerson. I wish to thank Dr. Stephen Williams for his helpful cooperation and encouragement, and Mrs. Iris Thomas for her aid in organizing the file material for shipment to New Mexico. The typing was done by Mrs. Elizabeth De Korne of Santa Fe, and the final stages of preparing the manuscript for publication were handled at the Peabody Museum by Burton J. Jones, director of publications, Emily Flint, editor, and Barbara Westman, staff artist. To my husband, Curt, I am grateful for his general assistance, sound advice, and patience during the preparation of this paper.

Polly Schaafsma
Arroyo Hondo, New Mexico
October, 1970

Donald Scott and His Collection

To hold in one's hand the result of a labor of love is highly rewarding. When that object is, at the same time, an important and historical contribution to a major field of research, the experience is unusual. Such is the fortune of the reader as he turns the pages of this monograph. The prehistoric rock art of Utah presented herein is a happy combination. The interest of a scholar, Polly Schaafsma, who has devoted recent years to the study of aboriginal art, has been applied to a unique collection of photographs and drawings. These are representations of petrographs, paintings, and carvings on rock, assembled by the late Donald Scott. He was first attracted to the "art galleries" on the cliffs and boulders of our American West in 1920. A vacation pack-trip in the rugged canyon and mesa country of southeastern Utah, then known to few save prospectors and Mormon cattlemen, produced a thread he was to follow for almost fifty years. His final additions to the collection were made only a few days before his death in 1967.

Donald Scott's career was extraordinary. He made his mark as businessman, publisher, scholar, and administrator, both governmental and academic, although he always maintained that his success as a cotton commission merchant in New York, the first job after college, left something to be desired. His achievements as a publisher are a matter of record: first, an editor, then secretary-treasurer, and later a director of the Century Company; a vice-president of the *New York Evening Post*; and the founder of the *Saturday Review of Literature*.

Throughout twenty-eight active years, of which the above highlights are merely an indication, a seed was germinating, planted before the turn of the century in his undergraduate days at Harvard, when the universities presenting anthropology as a formal subject could be counted on the fingers of one hand.

When Scott retired from business in 1928, the lure of trails on narrow eyebrow ledges hundreds of feet above the Colorado River, and the rock drawings of square-shouldered men or gods on the sheer red cliffs of Wingate and Navajo sandstone, drove him, paradoxically, back to Cambridge. He determined that future trips to the canyon country would have a purpose.

So, enrolled as a graduate student in the Peabody Museum, he renewed his acquaintance with Alfred M. Tozzer, Roland B. Dixon, A. V. Kidder, and Samuel J. Guernsey and, with customary energy set out to master the archaeology of the American Southwest and the Mountain States.

The attempt to escape the world of affairs was not a complete success. Dr. Edward Reynolds, a retired obstetrician, working under Earnest A. Hooton on the evolution of the pelvis from ape to man, had been tapped by President Lowell to succeed C. C. Willoughby as Director of the Peabody Museum. It did not take long for Dr. Reynolds to avail himself of Donald Scott's administrative ability and before he had been a graduate student for a year, our would-be scholar found himself appointed Assistant Director of the Museum. In that capacity, his experience acquired through the years in New York and Washington was very useful in helping to bring the Museum into the modern world. At the same time, his executive skill was such that he could keep the office to a part-time job, while his academic program did not suffer.

This was also the time when Noel Morss was developing his concept of the Fremont Culture in eastern Utah, the very area where Scott's deepest interests lay. William H. Claflin and Raymond Emerson had hatched their scheme for an archaeological reconnaissance of eastern Utah from the Arizona border to the Wyoming line, and Guernsey and Kidder were completing their studies of the Basketmaker caves of northeastern Arizona.

Naturally, all this coalesced and the western field trips continued, now with scientific purpose and a long-range plan. Morss, Claflin, and Emerson also were pack-train men. The Dirty Devil, Nine Mile Creek, Waterpocket Fold, Barrier Canyon, Jones Hole, and all the onetime haunts and rendezvous of Kit Carson and the Mountain Men came to know them well, and these surprising easterners came to know and record the archaeological sites and the pictures on the canyon walls.

Working together sometimes, more often on their own, they succeeded in covering a tremendous amount of country which was totally inaccessible to the ordinary person — and despite uranium prospecting and missile target sites, it still is.

Although Scott did little formal teaching, he generously took young students with him on many of his trips. There are senior archaeologists today and leaders in varied fields, including the business world, who learned clear thinking, practical or scientific method, and self-reliance from Donald Scott on the slick-rock trails, the muddy river fords, and the mini-deserts of eastern Utah.

He had, however, two constant assistants and companions who supported him as only good "seconds" can, throughout the many years of arduous but enjoyable and rewarding fieldwork. His wife, Louise Smith Scott, from Concord, Massachusetts, in addition to being a poet and president of the first graduating class at Simmons College, is a good horsewoman and a competent draughtsman. She served as an auxiliary beast of burden for the four to six still and movie cameras that her husband insisted on taking into places barred even to a rock-climbing Mormon mule. She did not have to carry binoculars or telescopes, however, because the first thing Guernsey taught Scott, which was the first thing he later taught me, was "Leave the binoculars in camp! They are useful for locating sites while riding along the trail, but if you are going to describe a site, you get there, close up, no matter how."

There is a story somewhere about Louise Scott in "the dead of night" (after dark, that is) typing notes on the typewriter of the blind postmaster and copying sketches of petrographs, to be put in the mail next morning in Escalante, Utah, then a very small town at the base of the Aquarius Plateau. One of the basic requirements of archaeological reconnaissance is that every time a post office is encountered, and this may be very seldom, copies of the notes must be posted for security in case the originals get dumped in the river, eaten by a Mormon rancher's goat, or just plain lost.

The second constant companion and the man who more than any other helped Donald Scott to "get there, no matter how," was the late Dave Rust. Born in Kanab, Utah, teaching school at the age of eighteen at Hanksville, and elected a year later to the state legislature, he was a true "native," with a boy's inquisitive interest in the Henry Mountains and the San Rafael Swell. His knowledge of the canyon country was encyclopedic. When, as a rank tenderfoot, I spent two months on the trail with him in 1931, he seemed to me to know everything about the geology, geography, flora, fauna, history, and folklore of the area. Forty years later, I still think he did.

Dave was the outfitter, guide, and mentor of most of our expeditions. He provided intimate knowledge of the country, the horses, and the mules; and his saddle mules were the smoothest-riding and best-trained quadrupeds I have ever met up with. He even had two mules broken to carry live mountain lions. If you have ever seen, much less had to handle, a bunch of stock which has somehow got the idea that there is a mountain lion within five miles, you will appreciate this point. Certain peculiar easterners have wished to bring back cubs alive, and some that had rather left off being cubs; so Dave, as the leading packer in the area, provided the mules that would carry them. The reader may be wondering what all this talk about mountain lions, well-trained, sure-footed mounts, etc., has to do with archaeology, science, or petrographs. Those who have been there will know.

It was Dave Rust who knew what "rock chimney" would lead to a particular cliff house, even though there was no obvious visual relationship. It was Dave who knew where and how to attach the rope that would give Scott access to a cliff house seventy-five feet below the rim of the canyon; or would enable him to photograph a petrograph panel, even though the ledge upon which the prehistoric artist had stood had long since crumbled away. I have a picture of D.S. with feet dangling, on his way up the "morning-glory" (otherwise "balanced") rock in Hill Creek on the East Tavaputs Plateau. One can be sure that such rocks will have an early site on top, and this one was no exception.*

The Utah fieldwork continued for many years and thousands of pictures were taken and drawings made. These, however, are only a part, albeit the most reliable and authoritative part of the huge Donald Scott collection. There is much more.

As he became acquainted with the field, and with the men who were or had been working in it, he began an extensive and ever-expanding correspondence. This not only produced items of information, ranging from those of high value to communications from the lunatic fringe, but brought to Cambridge thousands of photographs, drawings, and rubbings, in a constant stream, a stream which, even four years after his death, has not yet quite dried up.

Such is the collection. Scott kept it in excellent order, with a cataloguer, Mrs. Iris B. Thomas. His

---

* Gunnerson, 1969, fig. 38A; also see the illustrations in that volume for other pictures of our Utah expeditions.

original plan was to work it up and prepare several publications upon it. Years before the computer came to Harvard he envisioned a statistical study.

He could not, however, divorce himself from his many other interests. He left a great legacy to his juniors which was: "Never assume an obligation or let your name be put on a Board of Trustees unless you are prepared to work for it or otherwise justify your membership." So, he continued to do his duty by his many commitments, but time was running out. During his last few years he came to admit that he would never find the time to analyze the extraordinary and unique mass of material in his petrograph collection. Rather, he devoted his final years to making certain that the collection should be left in good order for future scholars to work up. This monograph by Polly Schaafsma is the first such work.

I say "first" advisedly, for although the area covered by this report was his favorite part of the West, the collection knows no geographical bounds. The Pueblo-Basketmaker materials to the south are well represented in the files, and are of second importance, scientifically and numerically; but the whole of our West is well covered, as are northern Mexico and western Canada. After these, which are the nucleus of the collection, come eastern North America and sporadic representation of rock art from the rest of the world.

Mrs. Schaafsma quite wisely decided, after viewing the collection as a whole, to spend her effort on its richest segment, the one Scott himself had emphasized. So we now have this magnificent presentation of Utah prehistoric rock art from the pen of one who appreciates and understands the motives and enthusiasm which directed the assembling of the collection.

Let me conclude this description of the collection and of the man who made it with a brief appraisal of the significance of rock art for the general archaeology of the region as it was developing while the collection was being formed. When Donald Scott was preparing for his serious studies, the foundations of archaeology and ethnology in the Southwest and Utah had been laid by such scholars as Fewkes, Cummings, Hewett, Kidder, Guernsey, and Judd. These men viewed the whole cultures of prehistoric and modern Indians and were interested in all aspects of their lives and times. There ensued a phase of increasing emphasis on taxonomy. The abundant pottery of the region is, of course, a very valuable index fossil for the study of both chronological and areal variations, but it lends itself so readily to taxonomic refinements that for a time its classification seemed to be regarded by some as almost synonymous with the delimitation of "cultures" rather than as one useful means to that end. From the start, however, Scott favored a balanced approach in which ceramic analysis plays its part but is not allowed to overshadow the study of architecture, agriculture, settlement pattern, and the arts and crafts other than pottery-making. He was interested in petrographs, in particular, not as an archaeological sideline but as potentially a very important avenue to the understanding of the social organization, ceremonialism, and even personal behavior of their creators. Although studies in the Old World had demonstrated that petrographs are a reliable source for prehistoric ethnology, Donald Scott was ahead of his time in believing that serious attention to petrographs could be equally rewarding for prehistorians of the American West. This monograph would seem to confirm his belief.

J. O. Brew
Peabody Museum
Cambridge, Massachusetts
February 14, 1971

The Rock Art of Utah

I

The Background

The state of Utah has been an area of long-standing archaeological interest and study, although recent years have shown a significant increase in the investigations in this area. Some of the earliest scientific reports on the state such as those by Mallery (1886 and 1893), Putnam (1876), and Dellenbaugh (1877) were concerned with its rock art. Early in this century, numerous archaeological sites, including rock carvings and paintings, were recorded and published by Reagan and Beckwith, while Steward included Utah rock art sites in more general publications on this subject (1929, 1937b) as well as in those reports dealing with Utah archaeology (1937a, 1941). Meanwhile, Judd (1926) discussed a significant number of rock paintings and carvings in his report on the archaeology of western Utah. In 1931, Morss published a report which recognized for the first time the existence of the Fremont culture, and this study included the most thorough consideration of Fremont rock art up to that time. Within the last two decades, the number of studies of Utah archaeology has in-creased, owing to the large areal surveys carried out by the University of Utah and the extensive salvage projects necessitated by dam building on the major rivers, in addition to numerous projects motivated entirely by research purposes. In all of these studies rock art sites have been consistently noted and the figures reproduced, and a few reports have been devoted entirely to a consideration of rock art alone. However, with a few exceptions such as Morss' work in 1931 and Turner's in the Glen Canyon (1963) and some discussion in general evaluation of Fremont culture by Wormington (1955), Gunnerson (1957, 1969) and Aikens (1967b), little attempt has been made to deal with Utah rock art as a tool for cultural analysis in conjunction with other archaeological data. It was thought that this objective might to some degree be accomplished with the Scott file material with its voluminous unpublished data, plus its documentation of the published material, all of which might be drawn together into a meaningful pattern.

DESCRIPTION OF THE STUDY

A preliminary review of the photographs led to the observation that the bulk of the Utah material is of Fremont origin. Major exceptions to this are the Virgin Kayenta petroglyphs and paintings in south-central and southwestern Utah and the Kayenta and San Juan Anasazi material in the southeastern part of the state. Other exceptions are the inclusions within the Fremont area of styles of probable non-Fremont origin, such as the Great Basin Abstract Style petroglyphs in western Utah. Since the Kayenta Anasazi rock art of Glen Canyon has already been studied in detail by Turner (1963), this data need not be reconsidered here. The San Juan Anasazi material from farther east, which was judged as being better considered in a separate study with related Anasazi rock art from Colorado and New Mexico, did not seem particularly relevant here in light of the Fremont em-phasis. An examination of the Virgin Kayenta data, however, did seem meaningful in light of possible Fremont-Virgin Kayenta relationships, and thus this Puebloan material has been included. It should be noted that the geographic span of the Fremont culture extends beyond the Utah borders into western Colorado on the east and into the eastern edge of Nevada on the west, while the Virgin Kayenta area encompasses not only southwestern Utah, but also the Arizona Strip to the south and the extreme southeastern portion of Nevada. It is natural that these areas should be included in this study.

It must be kept in mind that the nature of the available data may greatly affect the results of any research. Rock art studies from primarily photographic sources are fraught with a number of disadvantages. The inability to examine the rock art panels firsthand often causes one to overlook significant details in representation or important aspects of technique. Furthermore, the size of the figures is rarely indicated. Another serious deficiency in the data is that, except in the case of some published material, they seldom include the descriptions of geographic features and of any material culture associated with the rock art which, if reported, might have shed light on its cultural significance or function. Fortunately, however, before the manuscript was finished, I did have the opportunity to visit a number of eastern Utah sites.

On the other hand, a study of such a vast number of photographs has certain advantages. The collection represented here is much larger than could be obtained normally within the scope of any one research project or by any investigator on his own. The large amount of visual material available makes possible a description of the rock art over a considerable area, in this case throughout most of Utah and into related parts of adjacent states, which in turn leads to the recognition and definition of rock art styles of specific regions. Such styles have been demonstrated to be of considerable significance in the reconstruction of the culture history of prehistoric peoples as they are coincident with patterns present in other cultural data and are particularly sensitive in reflecting outside influences and contacts (Turner 1963, Schaafsma 1963). Thus one of the major outcomes of this study has been the definition of rock art styles throughout the areas under consideration and the additional light thrown thereby on current questions concerning the development and outside relationships of the Fremont and Virgin Kayenta cultures.

THE CONCEPT OF STYLE

Heizer and Baumhoff (1962) in their study in the Great Basin of eastern California and Nevada isolated five rock styles by means of a statistical inventory of the presence of definable elements. This stylistic analysis based on elements was successful and proved effective when used for the rock art in the Great Basin. Difficulties arise, however, when it is applied outside of this area, in 1) cases in which the same elements appear in several styles but which are distinguishable on a typological basis and 2) instances in which the same elements occur over a wide area but which show regional variations in attributes, frequency of occurrence, organization, and total aesthetic impact.

Following Heizer and Baumhoff's study, Turner (1963) in his petroglyph research in the Glen Canyon of northern Arizona and southern Utah very successfully distinguished five successive styles within this region. In this case, it was obviously necessary to take into consideration not only the elements or designs present in a given style, but also the techniques employed, the figure types, and to some degree the significant forms used as design components. In the Glen Canyon, Turner was able to date his five styles on the basis of pottery types found associated with petroglyph panels. Confusion with the style concept arises only in a later part of his paper where he makes his stylistic categories coequal with given time periods, and disregards in part his previous analysis of the style characteristics as he attempts to trace the existence of these styles outside of the Glen Canyon region. Perhaps, however, this latter aspect of his usage of style is somewhat irrelevant here, and it is mentioned only to avoid confusion in interpreting his work. It is his successful and comprehensive usage of the concept of style within Glen Canyon itself which should be stressed.

It would be worthwhile, perhaps, to reexamine the meaning of the concept of style divorced from any particular context and then to attempt to set up workable criteria for its use in rock art studies. If certain criteria of style can be agreed upon, they will immediately clarify the usage of the style concept and associated terminology in the current paper. Pertinent to this exploration of the meaning of "style" are certain aspects of Schapiro's consideration of the subject (1953, pp. 287–312). Schapiro states that the characteristics of styles vary continuously and resist systematic classification into perfectly distinct groups, but that precise limits are sometimes fixed by convention for simplicity in dealing with historical problems or in isolating a type. Furthermore, he points out that common to the approach of the art historian or anthropologist is the assumption that every style is peculiar to a period of culture and that in a given culture or epoch of culture, there is only one style or at least a limited range of styles. Therefore, style can be used with confidence as an independent clue to time and place of origin of a work of art (1953, p. 288). This position supports assumptions I have made in the present investigation.

More specifically, Schapiro states that "For the archeologist, style is exemplified in a motive or pattern, or in some directly grasped quality of the work of art, which helps him to localize and date the work and to establish connections between groups of works or between cultures" (1953, p. 287). Furthermore, style is studied more often as a diagnostic means by the archaeologist, than for its own sake as an important constituent of culture. The applicability of this to the current study is obvious. Certain clarifications need to be made, however, to accommodate his criteria of style to rock art studies in particular. For example, to quote, "By style is meant the constant form — and sometimes the constant elements, qualities, and expression — in the art of an individual or a group," or he more explicitly states that the description of a style refers to three things: 1) the form elements or motives, 2) form relationships, and 3) the qualities present including an overall quality which we may call expression. He adds that technique, subject matter, and material may be characteristic of certain groups and included in definitions of style, but are more often not so peculiar to the art of a period as are its formal and qualitative attributes (1953, pp. 287–289).

Let us first consider the characteristics of technique and subject matter, both of which are mentioned by Schapiro as being secondary considerations in the definition of style. It was clearly demonstrated in the case of the Glen Canyon rock art that the technical qualities of the petroglyphs did in fact vary consistently between the styles present in this region, and thus in this case, technique was considered a useful tool in distinguishing between styles, if not necessarily a major aspect of the styles themselves. In regard to content, again, most archaeologists involved in rock art studies would agree that an element inventory is also highly useful in distinguishing between rock art of different cultural groups. Stylistic considerations as such, however, fall into a more complex realm as defined above by Schapiro. Thus, important in a consideration are the major motifs, as well as the forms employed, which lead to the

development of basic recognizable figure types. Finally, the relationships between the various forms and subsequent figures in a panel lead to the creation of an overall aesthetic quality of expression which in many instances is an important aspect of style in rock art as it is in other realms of art. In the determination of any rock art style these numerous criteria must be constantly employed, and the value of these criteria may vary in importance from style to style. Thus the degree and rigidity of the use of these factors must be left up to the discretion of the investigator, depending upon the nature of the material with which he is working.

In the current study, the major stylistic categories were preliminarily determined by a rough sorting of the photographs according to their general appearance and on the basis of an intuitive evaluation of the elements present. With minor modifications the general validity of these categories was later substantiated, and the groups were refined by an objective analysis of the elements combined with a careful consideration of the techniques employed and of the aesthetic qualities present.

The elements and their frequency of occurrence have been tabulated, and a consideration of figure types and other attributes has been of prime importance as they show significant variation from area to area (tables 1–6). Aesthetic factors relating to the appearance of recurrent forms, the placement of figures or form relationships, and the overall expressive qualities characteristic of the various styles are discussed in the text.

Throughout this paper, a few terms are used in connection with style discussions for which definitions should be established. *Element* refers to any definable petroglyph figure. *Type* is the specific form and characteristic mode of expression of any element. The word *form* is used to refer to shape or configuration; while *motif* signifies a major theme, figure, or design used repeatedly.

THE GEOGRAPHIC AND CULTURAL SETTING

The Fremont and the Puebloan Virgin Kayenta cultures of Utah and adjacent regions encompass two physiographic provinces, the Colorado Plateau and the Basin and Range (fig. 1). These two major areas are sharply separated in central Utah by a range of high plateaus in the south and central portions and the Wasatch Range in the north, both of which exceed 10,000 feet in elevation in some spots. The Colorado Plateau of the eastern

Fremont and Virgin Kayenta regions is characterized by numerous mesas and plateaus, distinguished by colorful horizontal beds of sedimentary strata and dissected by deep river gorges and their tributary canyon systems. The variation in elevation determines the various climatic conditions which prevail. The coolest areas are the higher mesa regions ranging from 5000 to 9000 feet, which receive sufficient rainfall to sustain

FIGURE 1 Map showing principal physiographic divisions of Utah and adjacent regions.

a pinyon and juniper forest and the associated flora of the Upper Sonoran zone. The lower elevations, on the other hand, are considerably warmer and manifest arid and semiarid conditions.

West of the central plateaus and ranges, the topography changes into the flat open valleys and isolated parallel fault-block ranges of the eastern edge of the Great Basin province, characterized by semiarid interior drainage basins. Three deserts occur in western Utah: the Great Salt Lake Desert, the largest and northernmost; the Sevier-Black Rock Desert of central western Utah; and the Escalante Desert in the south (not to be confused with the Escalante River drainage of southeastern Utah). The western portion of the Virgin occupation and the western division of the Fremont culture area occupy this territory.

The Virgin culture is regarded as basically a variant of the Kayenta Anasazi. This will be discussed in more detail under the section dealing with Virgin Kayenta rock art. With the possible exception of certain northern fringe regions, most of Utah and the adjacent portions of Nevada and Colorado north of the Puebloan occupation are now generally regarded as the province of the Fremont culture. Substantial arguments have been put forth in recent years in favor of abandoning the term "Northern Periphery" for this area, and the term "Puebloid" for the more advanced archaeological manifestations in western Utah, and it seems reasonable to accept these proposals here without having to reiterate the arguments (Jennings and others 1956, p. 104; Taylor 1957, p. 162; and Ambler 1966a, p. 273). The internal diversity in the area now recognized as Fremont has been apparent for some time. Major divisions within the area were first outlined by Steward (1933a) and a similar scheme was later proposed by Wormington (1955). More recent schemes based on further research have been proposed by Ambler (1966a), Jones (1961), and Marwitt (1970).

With certain major exceptions in the Fremont west of the Wasatch (Marwitt 1970), most of these schemes are in large part consistent with that originally proposed by Steward.

Early in this investigation, the various Fremont rock art styles emerging from the study of the Scott file data were grouped by their geographic distributions. As a result, the Fremont east of the Wasatch was divided into three major zones (fig. 2) which were found to correspond with slight modifications to Ambler's Uinta Fremont and his northern and southern San Rafael sections (Ambler 1966a, fig. 51). Thus Ambler's terminology was adopted to describe the stylistic shifts in Fremont rock art in eastern Utah. West of the Wasatch Mountains, Fremont rock art is less evenly represented and the styles emerging from the data at hand, with the possible exceptions of paintings from Nevada sites (see Ambler's Conger Fremont 1966a), do not appear to follow regional divisions suggested by other investigators.

II

Rock Art East of the Wasatch Mountains

The Fremont area of eastern Utah includes the northwestern portion of the Colorado Plateau from the Uinta Range in the north, to the Escalante River, a tributary of the Colorado, in the south, all of which is drained by the Colorado River and its major tributary, the Green (fig. 2). The western boundary is clearly defined by the high ranges of central Utah. The eastern edge of the Fremont extends into western Colorado from the vicinity of the Yampa to the region around the Colorado River near its entry into Utah. South of here, the boundary is more or less determined by the Colorado River itself, although an inter-fingering of Anasazi and Fremont sites has been noted just east of the river, as well as west of it south of the mouth of the Dirty Devil.

The presence of Fremont sites throughout this area has been well established through numerous archaeological investigations, and an excellent summary of this material can be found in Wormington (1955, pp. 136–159). In addition to the Fremont culture and the Anasazi infiltration in the southern and eastern portions, there is indication of a sparse hunting and gathering Desert Culture or pre-Fremont occupation of this eastern Utah region that persisted until the Fremont culture became dominant, although findings of sites of probable Desert Culture origin have been scanty (Gunnerson 1957, p. 4, and 1969, p. 181; Breternitz 1970).

It is thus not surprising that we should find throughout eastern Utah a rock art configuration

also identifiable as Fremont. The Fremont tradition is characterized by the presence of a distinctive type of dominating anthropomorphic figure with a large head and a broad-shouldered, basically trapezoidal torso. In some regions, this figure is highly elaborated with necklaces and body decoration and complex headgear. Other large elements appearing in these panels are circular devices usually recognized as shields, although huge concentric circles and spirals are also popular. Mountain sheep are the most frequently depicted animals, although bison and deer are represented at many sites. Animal figures, often found in association with small anthropomorphic hunters, are small and simple for the most part, and both hunters and animals lack the development in design and technique manifested by the large Fremont anthropomorphs. There is also a wealth of abstract elements occurring in Fremont panels. Within this general Fremont configuration, regional variations and stylistic developments demand consideration and form the basis for the regional divisions mentioned earlier.

In addition, there are within the eastern Fremont area a number of specialized developments and rock art styles distinct from the generally recognized Fremont pattern, and these will be considered after the major Fremont configuration and its stylistic variants have been described. Of major importance here are the impressive Barrier Canyon Style paintings whose cultural affiliations are still held in question.

THE UINTA FREMONT

Within the Uinta Fremont region, rock art sites have been documented from two major districts (fig. 2). Of prime importance are the sites from the Vernal-Dinosaur district in the north. The Scott files document more than 100 petroglyph panels from the Ashley and Dry Fork Valleys alone. The records also include sites to the east along the Green and Yampa River drainages in Dinosaur National Monument. Figures from some of these

sites have been published by Reagan (1933a and b, and 1935). This district is outstanding not only in the variety and wealth of the Fremont rock art found there, but also in its unusual stylistic development of the Fremont theme. It is suggested that the term "Classic Vernal Style" be used to designate the distinctive style of Fremont rock art peculiar to this section of the Green River drainage. Secondly, from near the Colorado

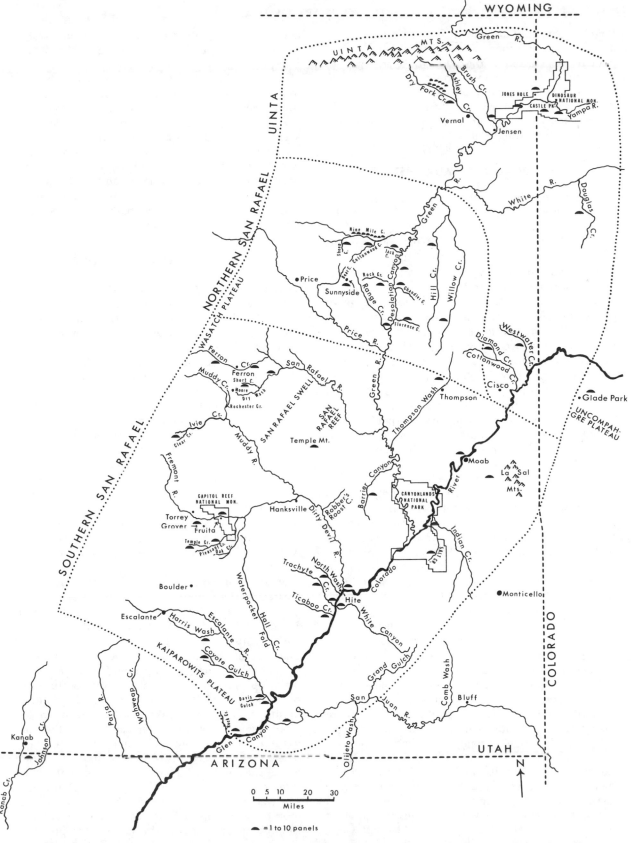

FIGURE 2 Map of Fremont area east of the Wasatch Mountains showing style zones, geographic details, and Fremont rock art site locations. Style zone boundaries and site locations are approximate.

River in east-central Utah near the Colorado line, and from the northern edge of the Uncompahgre Plateau in western Colorado, rock art sites of Fremont origin have been noted in previous publications (Wormington 1955, Lister and Dick 1952, Beauvais 1955, and Wormington and Lister 1956). These sites will be given new consideration here in light of additional data.

THE VERNAL-DINOSAUR DISTRICT

The large number of sites on record from the Vernal-Dinosaur district makes it possible to describe the rock art there with a fair degree of accuracy. Tables 1 and 2 present lists of elements and their major attributes from Classic Vernal Style sites in the Ashley and Dry Fork Valleys near Vernal and in Dinosaur National Monument, respectively. The tabulation of the percentage of occurrence of each element and attribute makes possible intraregional comparisons between the two localities as well as interregional stylistic comparisons later on. Before giving due consideration to the data presented in the tables or to the other stylistic properties present in the Vernal-Dinosaur rock art, however, a number of generalizations can be made in regard to its technical aspects.

With few exceptions, most of the rock art in this district occurs as petroglyphs which exhibit an unusually high standard of technical excellence as well as an interest in the effects of design. Large outline figures are preferred over solidly pecked elements, although the latter occur in panels of smaller figures for which this method of representation becomes more feasible. A variety of textural effects was achieved by different methods of manipulating the rock surface. In addition to pecking, the most commonly used technique, rubbing, abrading, and incising of the surface are also present. In one instance, a bas-relief carving occurs. Another method of figure definition evident in at least one Utah site and in two Colorado sites was the drilling or pecking of small holes in closely spaced rows to produce a stippled effect. This technique, however, seems to have been fairly limited both in use and in geographic range.

Painted designs are rather uncommon. There may have been, however, more painted designs originally than now remain, and painting seems to have been done in conjunction with petroglyphs. Reagan (MS. on file, Museum of New Mexico) mentions the presence of traces of red paint with Classic Vernal Style figures. He also notes paint remains in association with a series of figures of which only certain features of headdresses, faces,

and necklaces, and body decoration and sashes are pecked. There are no carved outlines, and today the figures have the effect of being very abstract or abbreviated representations of the Fremont anthropomorph. It is possible that once these designs were completed with painting. Examples of anthropomorphs of this type may be seen in figure 3. From Jones Hole in Dinosaur National Monument, there are anthropomorphs which are basically painted representations but which have pecked necklaces and body decoration. Other painted human figures, quadrupeds, and miscellaneous designs have been recorded from sites 42Un44 and 42Un68 in Dinosaur.

THE CLASSIC VERNAL STYLE

Barring certain distinct exceptions which will be considered in due course, most of the rock art in the Vernal-Dinosaur district is classified in this category, which embraces the most advanced expression of Fremont petroglyphic art. In their most extreme form, the panels of this style are characteristically forceful and imposing and composed of grand human figures with broad shoulders and large heads (figs. 3–6 and pls. 1–5). Such figures occur in 83 percent of the Ashley and Dry Fork sites and in 73 percent of the Dinosaur sites. The Vernal-Dinosaur artist was highly concerned with decorative effects and the elements of design, which in most instances take on a geometric quality. Thus, he took considerable interest in the depiction of precise ornamental detail, as well as in the overall effects created by the juxtaposition of angular and circular forms which heighten the compelling nature of these panels.

Small anthropomorphic figures, quadrupeds, and abstract designs are often found in the panels with the large dominating anthropomorph, although in 38 out of 83 Ashley-Dry Fork sites the large human figure occurs alone. Small anthropomorphic figures, typologically distinct from the large human representations, are found in 22 sites, but make up only 10 percent of the total occurrences of elements (table 1). Quadrupeds are found in 26 of the 99 sites and make up 19 percent of the total element inventory, indicating that they are more numerous than the small anthropomorph when they do occur. Abstract elements are found in 42 sites but make up only 24 percent of the total element inventory. In the Dinosaur sites, small elements accompanying the large anthropomorph are somewhat more widely distributed throughout the panels. The large anthropomorph

FIGURE 3 Classic Vernal Style petroglyphs, Ashley-Dry Fork Valleys. Source: Reagan-Nusbaum photo, Panel P 74.

FIGURE 4 Classic Vernal Style petroglyphs, Ashley-Dry Fork Valleys. Source: Reagan-Nusbaum photo, Panel P 30.

FIGURE 5 Classic Vernal Style petroglyphs, Ashley-Dry Fork Valleys. Source: Reagan-Nusbaum photo, Panel P 35. A fluteplayer appears beneath the third figure from the left in this panel.

FIGURE 6 Classic Vernal Style petroglyphs, Ashley-Dry Fork Valleys. Source: Reagan-Nusbaum photo, panel P 72. Probably the most elaborately carved Fremont panel in existence, the figures are largely incised, making possible the fluid outlines and a variety of textural effects. The anthropomorph to the viewer's right of the main figure is actually carved in bas-relief. According to Reagan's notes the figures were originally painted and some paint still remains. He also states that the panel is situated 100 feet above "any possible approach at the present time."

PLATE 1 Classic Vernal Style anthropomorphs, Ashley-Dry Fork Valleys. Figures are life-size. Reagan-Nusbaum photo, Panel P 34 a.

PLATE 2 Classic Vernal Style anthropomorphs with shield figures, Ashley-Dry Fork Valleys. Reagan-Nusbaum photo. Panel P 17.

PLATE 3 Classic Vernal Style anthropomorphs holding heads and shields, McKee Spring, Dinosaur National Monument (42Un89). Breternitz photo.

PLATE 4 Classic Vernal Style anthropomorphs, Ashley-Dry Fork Valleys. Figures are life-size. Reagan-Nusbaum photo, Panel P 39 a.

PLATE 5 Classic Vernal Style anthropomorphs, Ashley-Dry Fork Valleys. Reagan-Nusbaum photo, Panel P 13.

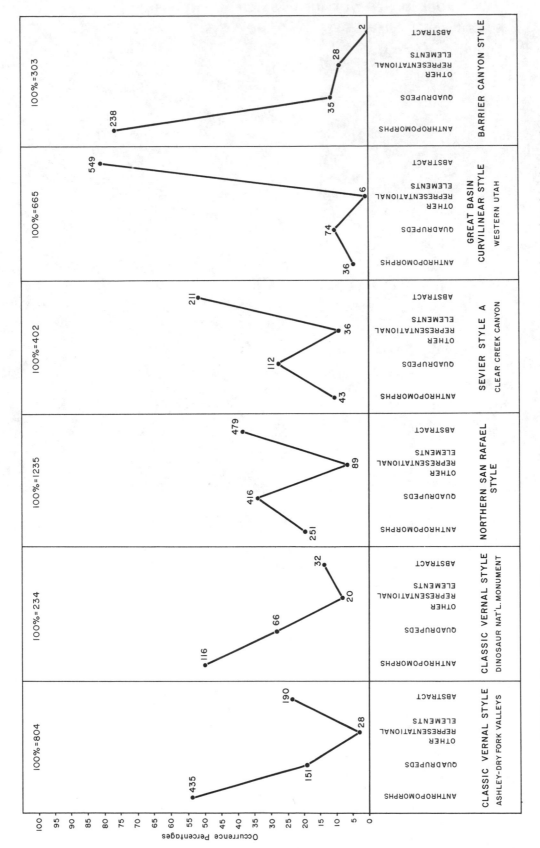

FIGURE 7 Chart showing profiles of occurrence percentages of major element categories of several Utah rock art styles.

rarely occurs alone here, yet small anthropomorphs, quadrupeds, and abstract designs make up only 12 percent, 28 percent, and 14 percent of the total element inventory respectively (table 2). Element occurrence percentages in Dinosaur sites are roughly in agreement with the Ashley and Dry Fork findings (fig. 7).

The Classic Vernal Anthropomorph. The Classic Vernal anthropomorph is characterized by a large trapezoidal body and a simple, large, round, rectangular, or bucket-shaped head (figs. 4–6 and pls. 1–5). The attributes of these figures have been enumerated in tables 1 and 2. In both Vernal and Dinosaur sites, outline figures occur with the greatest frequency, although solidly pecked figures occur with almost equal popularity in Dinosaur sites. The possibility was discussed above that figures lacking outlines, as do 23 percent of those in Ashley and Dry Fork sites and 15 percent of those in Dinosaur sites, were once completed by painting.

The torso of these figures is generally stylized and stiff, although a more naturalistic configuration is found among a small proportion of the Ashley and Dry Fork depictions (pl. 2, lower left). Barring the few naturalistic renditions, arms and legs, if present, are suggested by a single or double line and hands are usually missing. Feet with toes, however, are more popular and sometimes great delight was taken in exaggerating this feature.

Although these anthropomorphs are delineated in simple angular outlines, they are often highly elaborated with decorative detail executed with precision and considerable finesse. Headgear is absent on a roughly equal proportion of the anthropomorphs in Dinosaur and the Vernal sites, but occurs in both locales as rakes, horns, so-called "helmets," and as variations on the inverted bucket theme (fig. 8). Numerous other variations that defy classification are also manifest, some of the most interesting of which are constructed of dot designs. Further head decoration consists of earrings or earbobs and facial designs. Tear-streaks, also known as the "weeping eye" motif, are the most usual elaboration of the latter sort. Facial features themselves are present on a relatively high proportion of the anthropomorphs from both locales. Necklaces also occur regularly and may consist of one or two strands of beads portrayed with dots or as heavier pieces resembling shaped stone or shell. Bone pendants shaped like the necklace pieces depicted in the petroglyphs have been recovered by Breternitz from Cub Creek

Phase sites in the eastern Uinta Basin (Breternitz 1970, personal communication). An equal number of necklaces are solidly pecked and have the aspect of a yoke or collar. In the more detailed figure, the torso may be decorated, and kilts, breech clout, and sash may also be depicted. Rectangular shoulder pieces (pl. 3) and fringed kilts are features appearing in Dinosaur sites but lacking in the Ashley and Dry Fork representations. Phallic figures are rare, although they do occur in some detail in a few instances (fig. 9).

The Classic Vernal anthropomorphs are occasionally represented standing in arcs or hoops (pls. 4 and 6). In the latter, they resemble the shield figures discussed below. They may also be portrayed carrying small shields (pl. 3, fig. 6) or what may be either masks or human heads (pls. 1 & 3, figs. 3, 4, 5, 12). The heads carried by these figures vary from being highly detailed to being simplified almost beyond recognition.

A small number of panels in the Ashley and Dry Fork Valleys are variants on the Classic Vernal theme. The anthropomorphs, characterized by helmet type or rakelike headgear, lack the usual necklace, and their trapezoidal form may be solidly carved or exhibit patterned body decoration, that is, simple designs created by the opposition of solidly carved and open areas (pls. 7 and 8). A few figures are even triangular in shape and are decorated with horizontal lines. Anthropomorphic representations tend to be rather complete and large feet and hands with outspread fingers may be depicted. Anthropomorphs of this subgroup are more commonly associated with smaller elements, including lesser anthropomorphic representations, hunt scenes, and abstract designs as well as large recurrent circular motifs in the form of spirals, concentric circles, and shield designs.

As mentioned earlier a technological specialization of the Classic Vernal anthropomorph is found in the Poole Canyon site of Dinosaur National Monument in northwestern Colorado, where this figure is defined by means of closely spaced small drilled holes or pits (Baldwin 1947, p. 34). Photographs in the Scott files by David A. Breternitz (1963–1964) also record these same figures (pl. 9) and, in addition, drilled or pecked dot design anthropomorphs from two other sites. Similar carvings are reported by Reagan (MS, pp. 44 and 62, on file, Museum of New Mexico) from sites in northeastern Utah, but the dot carvings are not visible in the designated photographs. Anthropomorphs in plate 9 wear complex headdresses which combine the inverted bucket motif with

FIGURE 8 Classic Vernal Style headdresses from Ashley-Dry Fork Valleys. Source: Reagan-Nusbaum photos.

PLATE 6 Classic Vernal Style anthropomorphs, McKee Spring, Dinosaur National Monument (42Un89). Breternitz photo.

PLATE 7   Petroglyphs, Classic Vernal Style variant, Ashley-Dry Fork Valleys.   Reagan-Nusbaum photo, Panel P 88 a.

FIGURE 9   Classic Vernal Style petroglyphs, Ashley-Dry Fork Valleys.   Source: Reagan-Nusbaum photo, Panel P 51.

PLATE 8   Petroglyphs, Classic Vernal Style variant, Ashley-Dry Fork Valleys, Reagan-Nusbaum photo, Panel P 75.

PLATE 9   Fremont anthropomorphs defined by drilling or pitting, Classic Vernal Style, Poole Canyon, Dinosaur National Monument, Colorado (5Mf88).   Breternitz photo.

what appear to be long feather plumes. Another has long curved antennalike horns. A number of necklaces are visible which consist of closely placed representations of large stones carved in negative relief. The elegance of form seen in these anthropomorphs and the fine textural effects created by the drilled holes and the beautifully carved necklaces manifest the high artistry of this style.

Within the Classic Vernal Style, special anthropomorphic motifs and typological variants appear in addition to the conventional broad-shouldered figures already described. At two Dry Fork Valley sites, twins are depicted, typologically similar to the standard anthropomorphic figure (pl. 2). More commonly portrayed are anthropomorphs with bodies hidden behind large round shields. These personages, nevertheless, manifest traits in common with the conventional anthropomorphs, both in the specific matters of head shape and headdress styles, as well as in the more general aspects of technical rendition and in the overall qualities of geometric design (figs. 10, 11, 12 and pl. 2). Shield figures occur in greater numbers in the Ashley and Dry Fork Valleys than in the Dinosaur locality.

Finally, certain panels, including one described in the next paragraph, illustrate large naturalistic men depicted in the simple outline form, a type sometimes employed in this style, as we saw earlier (figs. 9, 13, 14). Those illustrated in figures 9, 13, and 14, however, are unusual in their profile view and in their bent posture.

Panels P 8 and P 76a. These two panels from the Dry Fork Valley containing unusual zoomorphs are of particular interest and merit separate discussion. In the first (fig. 14), the naturalistic man shown in profile as described above is engaged in a kind of dance reminiscent of the Bear Dance still done among the modern Utes. In the second panel (pl. 10), a bearlike creature appears to be dancing with a long-beaked bird, and another animal, probably a porcupine, is represented. It is interesting to notice that the four large zoomorphs present in these two panels embrace the typological extremes seen in the Classic Vernal anthropomorphic figures. The bearlike animals are pecked in simple naturalistic outlines, while the bird and porcupine are highly stylized with circular bodies and other geometric attributes.

In the second panel described, the zoomorphs are intersected by Classic Vernal anthropomorphs. The order of superimposition is not clear, although Reagan states in notes accompanying the photo-

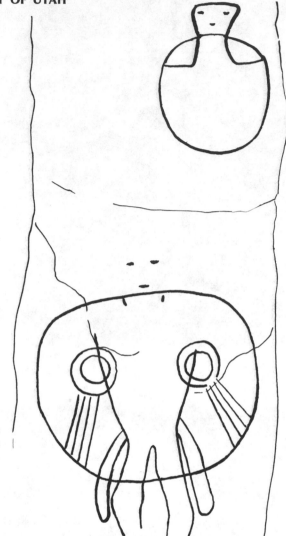

FIGURE 10   Classic Vernal Style shield figures, Ashley-Dry Fork Valleys. Source: Reagan-Nusbaum photo, Panel P 12.

graph that the anthropomorphs are carved over the animal dancers. Since they are stylistically similar, however, one would judge that not much time had elapsed between their execution.

Other elements present in these panels deserve consideration. In plate 10, long arrows and a flute player are depicted. Arrows are found on occasion in other Classic Vernal Style panels (fig. 15). Out of a hundred or so Ashley and Dry Fork panels, flute players occur in four instances and are shown with a curvilinear or nearly stick-figure body configuration. Two other examples from Dinosaur, however, are depicted upright and with angular bodies in keeping with the more conventional mode of anthropomorphic representation (fig. 16).

The small solid zoomorphs appearing in plate 10 are not distinctive, as figures of this type are portrayed in all Fremont regions. In figure 14 a maze, spiral, scorpion, and one-pole ladder are illustrated, all of which appear from time to time in other panels of this style. The precision with which they are carved and the wide spacing of these elements is characteristic of the clarity of the Classic Vernal Style.

Minor Elements Occurring in the Vernal-Dinosaur Panels. In addition to the maze, spiral, scorpion, and one-pole ladder discussed above, other elements make an occasional appearance in association with Classic Vernal Style anthropomorphs. Asterisks or small equilinear crosses, small circles with dots, and large concentric circles which may be spoked or segmented (fig. 3) may occur singly or in a typically uncrowded context. At one Vernal site, a winged anthropomorph with an owlish aspect is depicted (fig. 17). Serpents, bear tracks, and human hand- or footprints also occur rarely, while small quadrupeds, usually solidly carved, appear with greater frequency. Many of these latter figures in the Ashley and Dry Fork Valleys are generalized in form, although deer and mountain sheep may be identified in certain panels. Mountain sheep constitute 25 percent of all quadrupeds in Ashley and Dry Fork Valley sites and 61 percent in Dinosaur sites. In the Dinosaur sites, bison are depicted in addition to the deer and sheep. The Dinosaur sites also boast lizard representations

FIGURE 11 Classic Vernal Style shield figure, Ashley-Dry Fork Valleys. Source: Reagan-Nusbaum photo, Panel P 52.

FIGURE 12 Classic Vernal Style petroglyphs, Ashley-Dry Fork Valleys. Source: Reagan-Nusbaum photo, Panel P 15.

PLATE 10   Classic Vernal Style petroglyphs with stylized animals, Ashley-Dry Fork Valleys.   Reagan-Nusbaum photo, Panel P 8.

FIGURE 13   Classic Vernal Style petroglyph, Ashley-Dry Fork Valleys.   Source: Reagan-Nusbaum photo, Panel P 41.

FIGURE 14   Classic Vernal Style petroglyphs, Dance Scene, Ashley-Dry Fork Valleys.   Source: Reagan-Nusbaum photo, Panel P 76.

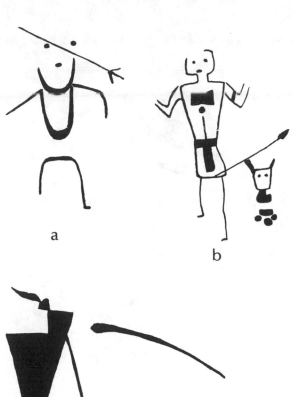

a

b

FIGURE 15 Classic Vernal Style anthropomorphs with arrows: a. Dinosaur National Monument, and b. Ashley and Dry Fork Valleys. Source: a, Breternitz photo, 42Un59. b. Reagan-Nusbaum photo, Panel P 48 c.

FIGURE 16 Fluteplayers, Dinosaur National Monument (42Un89). The figure on the left is over three feet tall. Source: Breternitz photo.

FIGURE 17 Winged anthropomorph, Classic Vernal Style. Near Vernal. Source: Reagan-Nusbaum photo, Panel P 54.

FIGURE 18 Lizard figures, Dinosaur National Monument (42Un59). Source: Breternitz photo.

FIGURE 19 Petroglyphs, Ashley-Dry Fork V
Source: Reagan-Nusbaum photo, Panel P 67.

(fig. 18). There is no way to determine if the lizards are contemporary with the other elements identified as Fremont, but one does note that they are carved with the same technical skill as figures of Fremont origin.

There are in the Ashley and Dry Fork Valleys a number of sites composed almost exclusively of small figures lacking the technical excellence and nicety of design found in most of the panels described above (figs. 19 and 20). Further study might justify a separate substyle grouping for these panels. The elements are highly varied and relatively crowded in arrangment. A few of these panels tend to resemble similar element assemblages from the northern San Rafael zone (fig. 20). Small anthropomorphs occur usually as stick figures or as solid representations. Approximately one-third of them are horned. Other elements include quadrupeds and the abstract designs enumerated in table 1, among which the maze is distinctive, although limited in number. Most popular among the abstract elements here are the wavy-line, concentric-circle, and spiral motifs. Definable abstract elements occurring in Utah sites are illustrated in figure 21.

OTHER STYLISTIC MANIFESTATIONS

There are on record a small number of sites and figures from the Vernal-Dinosaur district which differ sharply from the work described above, and which are not documented in tables 1 and 2. Among these is the Glen Canyon Style 5 panel which is discussed on pages 62–65 of this paper. In a couple of instances in the Ashley and Dry Fork Valleys, stick-figure men occur painted in red. In one case a large petroglyph panel of Fremont anthropomorphs is flanked by a red stick figure at each end. One of the painted men is nearly two feet tall. Another panel, 42Un77 (Gunnerson 1957, p. 43), displays a row of sixteen figures, eight of which carry round objects (fig. 22). Petroglyphs, including a Fremont anthropomorph, are scattered nearby. A third site displays asterisks and rows of short lines painted in light brown.

Colorado sites 5Mf134 and 5Mf175 in Dinosaur National Monument contain incised figures, among which are wandering lines, bear tracks, and circle motifs. Pecked footprints also occur, and there is a small group of painted designs, most of which cannot be identified.

NORTHWESTERN COLORADO

Following the Fremont province eastward into Colorado along the Yampa drainage, we find that, with the exception of the Classic Style dot figures in Poole Canyon and vicinity, rock art identifiable as Fremont seems to disappear, at least on the basis of the current data. Anthropomorphs from Castle Park only vaguely approximate the Fremont type. There are numerous human figures with trapezoidal bodies and small heads which more resemble Basketmaker anthropomorphs and lack specific Fremont elaborations such as complex headdresses, and necklaces. Other elements from this region are small double anthro-

FIGURE 20   Petroglyphs, Ashley-Dry Fork Valleys. Source: Reagan-Nusbaum photo, Panel P 79.

wavy line ∿∿∿∿

straight line ———

wandering line or
    curvilinear meander

rectilinear meander

zigzag ⋀⋁⋀⋁⋀⋁

enclosing wavy lines

spiral

double spiral

rectilinear spiral

spiral with wavy line

circle ○

spoked or segmented circle

bisected circle ⊘

tailed circle

concentric circle ◎

circle with dot ⊙

sun disc

chain of circles ○○○○

connected circles

triangle △

lozenge chain ◇◇◇ ◇◇◇◇

rake ⊓⊓⊓

convoluted rake

sawtooth △△△△△

one-pole ladder

two-pole ladder

scorpion

plant form

dot or dot design ···· ⋮⋮⋮

row of short lines | | | | | |

nested chevron ⋘⋘

bird track ⟨

deer hoof

asterisk or cross ＊   ＋

maze

enclosed decorated area

rectangular grid

abstract face or mask

FIGURE 21   Chart of illustrated examples of abstract elements enumerated in the cumulative data tables.

pomorphs, suggestive in subject matter, if not in type, of the Fremont twins, plus mountain sheep, birds, animal tracks, and footprints (Burgh and Scoggin 1948, fig. 44).

Farther south, along Douglas Creek in the White River drainage, where Fremont occupation is evidenced by architecture, pottery, and other artifacts, pictographs are reported of which the dominant type was a trapezoid-bodied anthropomorph similar to those found by Morss in the Fremont drainage. Of the twenty-eight examples found, eighteen were horned (Report of Gilbert R. Wenger given in Wormington 1955, p. 142).

SOUTHERN UINTA SITES NEAR THE COLORADO RIVER

A small number of sites have been documented in the literature from west-central Colorado and east-central Utah in the vicinity of the Colorado River. A Sieber Canyon site near Glade Park just beyond the Uinta region border as shown in figure 2 has been reported by Lister and Dick (1952), Beauvais (1955), and Wormington and Lister (1956). The dominant element here is the Fremont anthropomorph with kilt, helmet-style headdress, and raketype horns or antlers. At least twenty-five examples of this figure were noted, and they ranged in height from 10 to 42 inches (Lister and Dick 1952, p. 92). These figures are very similar typologically to the variant on the Classic Vernal anthropomorph described on page 15 and illustrated in plate 7. Associated are wavy lines, snakes, circles, and spirals, plus the bear track, a prevalent element in Colorado sites.

A few other sites are recorded from the Uncompahgre Plateau, but as they are not characteristic of the Fremont culture and are varied in style and few in number, they cannot be meaningfully discussed at this time. The grooved lines and bearpaw representations from the Moore Shelter may date from the earlier Uncompahgre Complex, a Desert Culture component (Wormington and Lister 1956, p. 78).

The Westwater and Diamond Creek Paintings. West of Glade Park along Westwater and Diamond Creeks of eastern Utah (fig. 2), there are several rock paintings possibly of Fremont origin which are discussed in some detail by Wormington (1955, pp. 79–85, figs. 49–52). These paintings are more or less stylistically homogeneous and totally distinct from the Fremont work heretofore described (figs. 23 and 24). None of the usual broadshouldered trapezoidal men are represented, but

FIGURE 22 Row of painted stick figures, Ashley-Dry Fork Valleys (42Un77). Figures are 0.3 feet tall. Source: Reagan-Nusbaum photo, Panel P 100B.

FIGURE 23 Painted shield bearer, Westwater Creek, Panel A. The shield figure is approximately four feet in height. Source: Wormington 1955, fig. 51, upper.

shield bearers are popular. There is one painting of a realistic owl. The shield men lack the traditional large heads and contained, static quality that is found in the northern figures. They characteristically are painted with longer legs denoting action, and in addition, long devices resembling spears project to some length from behind the shields. Although it is sometimes difficult to compare pecked and painted work, the absence of the familiar Fremont anthropomorphs and the general fluid quality present in the figures described, as well as the accompanying linear elements, suggest that these figures are a local manifestation of Fremont rock art.

In sum, it is suggested that future investigations in this eastern edge of the Fremont area may indicate the necessity for the creation of a separate style zone in this region. Such a zone would encompass sites not only in the Westwater Creek-Glade Park districts, but also sites farther south in the vicinity of Moab and the La Sal Mountains (see below, p. 53). Affinities to the northern Uinta stylistic configuration are evident in figure types shared between the Classic Vernal Style variant described on page 15 and anthropomorphs from Seiber Canyon, Moab, and the La Sal Mountains. It also appears that this entire region is further united by the representation of animal tracks, an element commonly found in western Colorado rock art sites.

FIGURE 24 Rock paintings, Westwater Creek, Panel B. The pecked horsemen on the right are noted by Worm-ington (1955, page 83) to be superimposed in part over the older red designs and are believed to be Shoshonean. Source: Wormington 1955, fig. 51, lower.

THE SAN RAFAEL FREMONT — THE NORTHERN ZONE

South of the Uinta Fremont region is the San Rafael region, which is divided into northern and southern zones (fig. 2). The most thoroughly documented drainage in the northern zone is Nine Mile Canyon and its tributaries, from which approximately one hundred rock art panels have been recorded. South of Nine Mile Canyon, ma-terial is on file from additional sites in Jack Canyon, Rock Creek, and Range Creek, all western tribu-taries of the Green River. Data are lacking from the Price River drainage south of Range Creek. In the current study, Ambler's northernmost boundary of the San Rafael region has been ex-tended eastward to include Hill and Willow Creeks, eastern tributaries to the Green. Other docu-mented eastern tributaries are Florence and Chandler Canyons. Panels from Desolation Can-yon on the Green River itself have been reported by Gaumer (1937, figs. 1 and 2), and one other Green River site is recorded in the files.

Element and attribute data from individual sites are recorded in table 3. Sites tabulated from Nine Mile Canyon consist of a representative sample of the total number of sites from this drainage, since many of the photographs did not show the petroglyphs clearly enough to be realistically in-corporated into the study. A small number of other sites are composed largely of figures of his-toric origin. The data indicate that as a group the petroglyphs and rock paintings in the above named canyons exhibit a stylistic phase of Fremont rock art which is internally consistent and distinct from that of the Uinta region and which can be differentiated from that of the southern San Rafael zone.

THE NORTHERN SAN RAFAEL STYLE

The rock art style of the northern zone of the San Rafael region stands in decided contrast to the northern Uinta region sites examined above. Lacking in the northern San Rafael are the panels composed of large, precisely executed trapezoidal men and shield bearers with their detailed ornamentation. With a few exceptions, an interest in the creation of pleasing visual patterns predominant in the Classic Vernal Style is gone. Instead, large and small panels are crowded and busy, with a wealth of small solidly pecked figures which may be carelessly executed and ill-defined. The average number of elements per panel is almost double that in the Ashley and Dry Fork work. Anthropomorphic figures constitute only 20 percent of the total element inventory in northern San Rafael sites as opposed to 54 percent (large and small anthropomorphs combined) of all elements in the Ashley and Dry Fork Valleys and 50 percent of the elements in Dinosaur panels (fig. 7). No distinction has been made between large and small anthropomorphs in table 3 since they grade together imperceptibly in northern San Rafael sites. In fact, large figures as such are extremely rare. In these panels the trapezoidal-bodied Fremont anthropomorph is on the average greatly reduced in size. Although an anthropomorphic figure may occasionally dominate the other elements, he lacks the commanding aspect of his northern cousins. He may be crowded by other figures or stripped of his gear to become simplified almost beyond recognition. Quadrupeds make up 34 percent of all elements as opposed to 19 percent in Ashley-Dry Fork sites and 28 percent in Dinosaur sites. Other small representative elements such as serpents, birds, shields, handprints, and tracks combine to make up another 7 percent. A significant increase over northern Uinta panels is shown among the abstract elements, which constitute 39 percent of the figures in northern San Rafael panels, as opposed to 24 percent in the Ashley and Dry Fork Valley petroglyphs and 14 percent in Dinosaur rock art. There is also an increase in the number of rock paintings occurring in the northern San Rafael zone. This is particularly noticeable in sites on the left bank tributaries to the Green River, where painted panels are equal in number to petroglyphs.

A more detailed description of the component elements in the northern San Rafael panels will aid in further defining the style of this zone.

Anthropomorphic Figures. As mentioned above, the large trapezoidal Fremont anthropomorph occurs only rarely and even more rarely does he appear alone. This figure is most often found in petroglyph form, although a few painted but simple representations occur along Range Creek and in the Nine Mile district. Elaborate paintings of "antlered warriors in black, white, red and yellow and up to three feet in height" have been reported from Florence Canyon (Murbarger 1960, p. 27).

The larger anthropomorphs exhibit a certain conformity to a typological norm, with a trapezoidal body and bucket-shaped head. The body form may be flared at the base to suggest a kilt. A few anthropomorphs are not elaborated much beyond this, although many of the figures of this type are portrayed with long rakelike horns or antlers, which curve either over the head or outward over the shoulders (figs. 25–27, and pl. 11). These figures have arms, which are commonly bent at the elbow, and hands with spread fingers. Legs are usually short and straight, and no examples of the foot exaggeration found among the northern Uinta anthropomorphs are present in the northern San Rafael material. Examples of masks or facial features are rare (fig. 28 and pl. 12). An occasional figure carriers a spear, and one appears to hold a small shield (fig. 25). Whatever these figures lack in austerity they gain in vitality conveyed through fringed headgear, jointed arms, and out-spread fingers, and through an occasional frenzied stance (fig. 26).

A few anthropomorphic figures display rectangular or triangular body shapes instead of the usual trapezoidal configuration (figs. 29 and 30). Shield men also occur, which have undergone the same reduction in size and the simplification seen in the diagnostic Fremont anthropomorphic type (fig. 30 and pls. 12 and 13). They are usually solidly pecked and are shown with bucket-shaped heads and horns.

The majority of anthropomorphs, regardless of size, are solidly painted or pecked. Exceptional among northern San Rafael anthropomorphs are outline figures from Nine Mile Canyon panel, NP 19 (fig. 31), and the Rock Creek Site (fig. 28). The first example depicts parts of three figures defined in outline resembling anthropomorphs in the Classic Vernal Style. The Rock Creek Panel shows other anthropomorphs reminiscent of northern Uinta work carved in outline with facial features and a necklace indicated.

FIGURE 25 Petroglyphs, probably Nine Mile Canyon. Source: Lewis B. Jones photo, J6.

PLATE 11 Petroglyphs, Nine Mile Canyon. The spiral in the upper left is two feet in diameter. Reagan-Nusbaum photo, Panel NP 7.

The smaller solidly pecked anthropomorphic representations display a considerable amount of typological variation. Some figures maintain echoes of the larger Fremont types in their broad-shouldered trapezoidal or more rarely triangular forms and in their horned headdresses. They sometimes appear as hunters and may be shown in an attempted profile or three-quarter view with bent legs and angled body (fig. 32 and pl. 14). Many small anthropomorphs have irregular and indefinite body forms pecked in the careless manner occurring in this region. Still others are reduced to crude stick-figure representations. All of these figures may carry bows with which they are shown hunting (fig. 33 and pls. 11, 12, and 14). It is notable that the fluteplayer is not represented in the file material from this zone. One panel shows anthropomorphs standing in hoops (fig. 34).

Examples of distinctive, small linear anthropomorphic figures found sporadically throughout the entire San Rafael region will be discussed below under "Specialized Developments," etc., page 60.

Quadrupeds. Animals appear singly or in groups in the majority of northern San Rafael panels, and among them the mountain sheep enjoys the greatest popularity. It should be mentioned here that the *intended* number of sheep is probably much greater than table 3 indicates, as only those animals with distinctively mountain sheep horns were included in the count. A large number of animals remain unidentified. Antlered figures representing deer or elk occur in a much higher ratio in northern San Rafael sites than in the northern Uinta sites. Finally, bison occur from time to time (fig. 35). The anthropomorphic hunters frequently

FIGURE 26 Petroglyphs, Nine Mile Canyon or Sunnyside. Source: Lewis B. Jones photo, J5.

FIGURE 27 Petroglyphs, Fortification Rock, Hill Creek Canyon, ET–6–7.

FIGURE 28 Petroglyphs, Rock Creek, a partial reconstruction. A rare example of Classic Vernal Style characteristics in Northern San Rafael work.

FIGURE 29 Petroglyphs, Nine Mile Canyon.

PLATE 12   Petroglyphs, Nine Mile Canyon. Claflin-Emerson Expedition photo.

PLATE 13   Petroglyphs, Nine Mile Canyon. The long serpent is ten feet in length. Reagan-Nusbaum photo, Panel NP 21.

associated with animal herds were discussed above, and in a few instances animals have been shot with arrows.

Among the quadrupeds, there are some typological variations which merit comment. Some animals are depicted with a surprising degree of naturalism, as seen in the bison in fig. 35. At certain Nine Mile Canyon and Willow Creek sites there are sheep, elk, and deer with relatively graceful curvilinear configurations pecked in outline or as solid forms (fig. 36 and pl. 15). The tendency toward a rounded posterior and a long,

outstretched neck is distinctive. The type is well exemplified at Site 31 (PR–4–31),* a rock shelter in Nine Mile Canyon containing Basketmaker and Fremont occupations (Morss 1931, and Gunnerson 1969). One painted example here is acephalous.

Compact stylized sheep are more typical of Fremont work (fig. 25). Those with crescent-shaped or strongly rectilinear bodies are often technically superior to other examples and may be shown with cloven hooves (figs. 32 and 37 and pls. 11, 12, and 16). All stages exist between these quad-

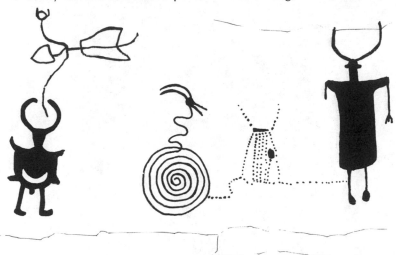

FIGURE 30 Petroglyphs, Nine Mile Canyon, PR–4–5.

FIGURE 31 Petroglyphs, Nine Mile Canyon. Source: Reagan-Nusbaum photo, Panel NP 19.

FIGURE 32 Petroglyphs, Sheep Canyon, tributary to Nine Mile. Source: Reagan-Nusbaum photo, Panel NP 23.

* Site designations of this nature are numbers assigned by the Claflin-Emerson expedition (Gunnerson 1969, p. 27). Prefixes refer to abbreviation of quadrangle name in which site occurs. Hence: FL — Fish Lake; SR — San Rafael; LS — La Sal; PR — Price River; U — Uinta; ET — East Tavaputs, etc.

PLATE 14   Petroglyphs, Nine Mile Canyon.   Hunt scene.   Reagan-Nusbaum photo, Panel NP 26.

PLATE 15 Red painting of deer or elk, Site 31, Nine Mile Canyon. Beckwith photo.

PLATE 16 Petroglyphs, Cottonwood Canyon, tributary of Nine Mile Canyon. Beckwith photo, Panel B 30.

FIGURE 33 Hunting scene petroglyph, Nine Mile Canyon. Source: Beckwith photo, Panel B 3.

rupeds and those technically inferior representations which may on occasion be reduced conceptually to stick figures. In some instances these latter quadrupeds undergo extreme elongation. All types appear together and their variations seem to have no cultural or chronological significance. Of special note is the appearance at three sites of mountain sheep with horns shown in frontal perspective rather than in the traditional profile (fig. 38). A rare example of a vertically depicted animal is shown in plate 17.

Serpents. Serpents as such appear in only thirteen of the northern San Rafael sites recorded in the files. We are concerned here with only those figures which are clearly reptilian and not those indistinguishable from wavy lines. Most commonly, the serpent appears as a wavy line of varied regularity with a loop or blob at the end to suggest a head (pls. 12 and 13 and figs. 30 left and 33). At three sites he is seen as a wavy line with a horned or plumed headdress (figs. 31 and 39). In another still more elaborate representation, the body is defined with double lines and the intermediate space is filled with diamond cross-hatching. This figure is also plumed (fig. 37). In another instance, the serpent is represented as a spiral, and the mouth and plumes are strongly emphasized (fig. 30).

FIGURE 34 Petroglyphs, Nine Mile Canyon.

FIGURE 35 Petroglyphs, probably Nine Mile Canyon. Source: Beckwith photo, Panel B 24.

FIGURE 36 Petroglyph of deer, Willow Creek. ET–10–4.

Other Representational Figures. There are few other representational elements. Three large circular painted designs are on record from Cottonwood Canyon, a tributary to Nine Mile, and these supposedly represent shields. Their decoration is simply conceived (Wormington 1955, fig. 63, i–l). Birds (fig. 37 and pl. 18) are depicted at only three sites. They have long legs and necks and appear to represent water fowl. In addition there is a rare animal track and an occasional human hand or footprint.

Abstract Elements. As mentioned above, abstract elements constitute 39 percent of the elements in the northern San Rafael sites. There are a few panels in which abstract elements appear almost exclusively (fig. 40). For the most part, however,

FIGURE 37 Petroglyphs, Nine Mile Canyon. Source: Beckwith photo, Panel B 23.

they occur in association with representative figures (pls. 11, 12, 13, 18, and 19; figs. 27, 29–30, 33, 35, 38, 39, and 41). Twenty-seven percent of the abstract elements defy classification. The remaining 73 percent are recurring designs which can be categorized. Among these, the wavy line shows the highest percentage of occurrence, making up 17 percent of these designs. The dot or dot design, plain circle, concentric circle, and wandering line are next in order of popularity representing 11 percent, 6 percent, 5 percent, and 5 percent of the abstract elements, respectively. These findings provide an interesting comparison with those of the Vernal-Dinosaur district, where, with a few exceptions, most of the same abstract figures occur. In the latter instance wavy lines and concentric circles also show a relatively high degree of popularity. Spirals, however, manifest a significantly higher percentage of occurrence in the Vernal-Dinosaur sites, while dots and dot designs show a substantial increase in the northern San Rafael zone. It should be noted that, owing to the lack of unclassifiable figures in the northern Uinta sites, the percentages given for the definable elements in the latter district are generally higher than those for the northern San Rafael zone.

PLATE 17 Petroglyphs, Nine Mile Canyon. Beckwith photo, Panel B 25.

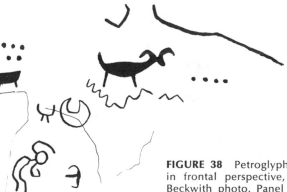

FIGURE 38 Petroglyph, mountain sheep with horns in frontal perspective, Nine Mile Canyon. Source: Beckwith photo, Panel B 1.

PLATE 18   Petroglyphs, Nine Mile Canyon. Reagan-Nusbaum photo, Panel NP 18 a.

FIGURE 39 Petroglyph panel emphasizing dot designs, Cottonwood Canyon, tributary to Nine Mile. Source: Beckwith photo, B 4.

PLATE 19   Petroglyphs, Nine Mile Canyon. Reagan-Nusbaum photo, Panel NP 2.

FIGURE 40   Petroglyph of abstract elements, Nine Mile Canyon, near PR–4–5.

FIGURE 41   Petroglyph, Fortification Rock, Hill Creek, ET–6–7.

THE SAN RAFAEL FREMONT — THE SOUTHERN ZONE

The southern division of the San Rafael Fremont as defined by Ambler (1966a, fig. 51), extends roughly from the San Rafael River and the mouth of the Green River in the north, south to the general vicinity of the Escalante and is confined to the right bank of the Colorado. For the current purpose of defining the areal distribution of Fremont rock art styles, the northern boundary is extended north and east to include the Fremont style rock paintings and petroglyphs at Thompson and Moab and on Salt and Indian Creeks in Canyonlands National Park on the left bank of the Colorado (fig. 2). The southern boundary is extended south and east to include Fremont rock art sites in a region which was occupied predominantly by the Kayenta Anasazi. The Fremont rock art from this entire fringe area is generally consistent stylistically with that of the greater southern San Rafael zone.

The documented locations from the southern San Rafael are widely scattered. In addition to those mentioned above, other site localities include the Ferron district, the eastern edge or reef of the San Rafael Swell, and the vicinity of the Green and Colorado Rivers and their tributaries from Barrier Canyon in the north, south to Ticaboo Creek. Of major importance are sites in the Fremont River district near Fruita, most of which have been previously discussed by Morss (1931).

Cumulative data charts were not made for the southern San Rafael sites, since they show a high degree of variation stylistically, and it was therefore felt that an individual description of each site or locality would be more appropriate. As opposed to the material on record for the northern San Rafael and the northern Uinta Fremont, the data on hand for the southern San Rafael represent only a few sites or panels from each of the above named locations. It is perhaps because of the wide and scattered distribution of the sites through the rugged terrain characteristic of the region, that the Fremont rock art in the southern San Rafael lacks the stylistic unity found to the north. Nevertheless, a few generalizations in regard to the rock art of this zone can be made.

In southern San Rafael sites, the distinctive Fremont anthropomorphic figure regains its position of dominance and manifests some of the elaboration and technical excellence found in the Uinta region. Complex headgear, facial decoration, and necklaces again appear, but with less variety and with characteristics peculiar to this southern region. Round hairbobs (or earrings?) are found on many southern San Rafael anthropomorphs. A

number of figures are characterized by a diagonal line drawn across the torso, which perhaps represents a carrying strap. The dot decoration so commonly employed on figures in the Uinta sites is only rarely seen in the southern San Rafael. Painted depictions are more prevalent in the latter region, and these paintings, especially those from the Salt Creek drainage, manifest an unusual number of traits characteristic of Fremont figurines. Among the attributes shared by the anthropomorphs of these two art forms are the persistent lack of appendages, the long, rounded, or extended chin and the tendency for both classes of figures to occur in pairs. The Salt Creek rock paintings show further likenesses in the presence of "shoulder bobs" and coffee-bean-like or slit eyes, and in body decoration.

"Shoulder bob" refers to a hair style exemplified by a Pueblo Indian skull from Tsegi Canyon, Arizona, and associated wall paintings in which "The long hair was wrapped with a cord about the thickness of a lead pencil made up of heavy strands of fibre string. This cord wraps both bobs, crossing from right to left on the nape of the neck" (Guernsey 1931, p. 94, plate 12, fig. 27). A similar arrangement, with the hairbob pressing down on the shoulders, is characteristic of the more elaborate Fremont figurines such as the Pillings group from Range Creek, Utah (Morss 1954). Although the skull excavated by Guernsey was that of a young woman and he suggested that it showed a "way in which the women of the Pueblo I period arranged their hair," a similar hairdo is shown on Fremont figurines and rock art figures representing both sexes.

Paralleling the standard Fremont anthropomorph in the southern San Rafael is the shield figure, which again is represented in some detail and on a relatively large scale. Although the proliferation of smaller solidly pecked elements including various quadrupeds and abstract designs has somewhat subsided in the southern San Rafael, we do find panels of these figures occurring separately or in association with the dominant anthropomorph. In some instances, the panels of small miscellaneous elements are stylistically indistinguishable from those of the northern San Rafael. One often notes, however, a technical improvement in the carving and an interest in the effects of form and design. Certain panels of these figures, especially those from the Ferron district, manifest local characteristics.

Further generalizations concerning the Fremont

rock art of the southern San Rafael zone as a whole are difficult because of the variety encountered in the various districts or river drainages. Thus it seems more profitable at this point to proceed with a description of specific sites or other intra-regional divisions, as the data dictate, in order to obtain a complete picture of the rock art of this zone.

THOMPSON WASH

The Fremont petroglyphs on Thompson Wash have been discussed by Morss (1931, pp. 38–40) and Gunnerson (1957, pp. 74–77). Two series of petroglyphs are superimposed upon large figures painted in red in Panel 1 of this site. The painted anthropomorphs are unadorned and have small insignificant heads. Over these is a series of fully pecked human figures with trapezoidal heads and bodies. One figure is horned. Over these are again superimposed two anthropomorphs in outline with typical Fremont treatment of the waist and necklace. Mountain sheep and various other designs interfere with the figures of the second series and appear to be as late as or later than the third series (Morss 1931, p. 39). Morss suggests that we have here stratigraphic evidence of a succession from Basketmaker or quasi-Basketmaker prototypes to Fremont rock art. This suggestion will be examined further under "Evidence for Chronological Developments within Fremont Rock Art."

THE FERRON DISTRICT

From the vicinity of Ferron, Utah, there are on record eight panels from four or more sites, which manifest their own distinctive qualities. At 42 Em39 on Ferron Creek, east of Molen, is a series of anthropomorphic figures in conjunction with animals and abstract elements (fig. 42). This panel is briefly mentioned by Gunnerson (1957, p. 145). The torsos of the human figures vary from trapezoidal to square in shape and display a characteristic v-shaped decoration. Other notable elaborations are the circular motifs commonly found in southern San Rafael sites, variously interpreted as hairbobs or earrings, and the short straight horns as headgear. These figures are depicted with arcs sweeping over their heads or shoulders, a motif found sporadically in northern San Rafael and Uinta sites. Other associated figures include wavy lines, dotted lines, and aggregates of diamond shapes resembling nets. Displayed here is a clarity and solidity of figure definition characteristic of other panels in the Ferron district. Undocumented in the Scott collection, but also present in Ferron Canyon, are twelve pecked sandal or moccasin prints described by Gunnerson (1957, p. 145) and two groups of Barrier Canyon Style paintings.

On Ferron Creek, west of Ferron, are petroglyphs (pl. 20) well carved in broad lines, of concentric circles, spoked concentric circles, zigzags, and sunbursts, as well as quadrupeds and anthropomorphs. The u-shaped rake and abstract mask or face element are unique in this site. Similar in aesthetic effect are petroglyphs from Short Canyon, east of Moore, of one-pole ladders, concentric semi-circles, circles with dots, and mountain sheep and Fremont anthropomorphs (pl. 21). In the latter case, the Fremont type designs are carved over red paintings which are unlike any others in this study, and which may not be of Fremont

FIGURE 42 Carved and painted Fremont figures on Ferron Creek (42Em39). The hatched areas are painted and the rest is carved. Source: Beckwith photo.

PLATE 20 Petroglyphs, Ferron Creek, west of Ferron. The wide line carvings are typical of the Ferron district. Beckwith photo.

origin. Barrier Canyon type figures are also present some distance away on the same ledge.

Other paintings from the Ferron district include a row of abbreviated, Fremont type, anthropomorphic forms with triangular torsos and bucket-shaped heads (pl. 22). Two more large painted human figures lacking the tidiness characteristic of other Ferron panels are found in association with a number of grids scratched in fine lines (pl. 23). The order of superimposition is not clear although the probability that the scratched designs are later is suggested by the presence of scratched antlers on one of the painted anthropomorphs (see p. 62).

SITE NEAR THE JUNCTION OF CLEAR AND IVIE CREEKS
(42Sv7)

A painted Fremont site is situated near the Old Woman site described by Taylor (1957, p. 81, fig. 30). The figures consist of four large horned anthropomorphs 45″ tall, shieldlike devices, animals, snakes, and hand prints.

THE FREMONT RIVER DISTRICT

The rock art of the Fremont River district as well as that from sites situated in the vicinity of the Colorado River between the mouth of the Dirty

PLATE 21 Fremont type petroglyphs superimposed over painted red designs. Short Canyon, east of Moore. Beckwith photo.

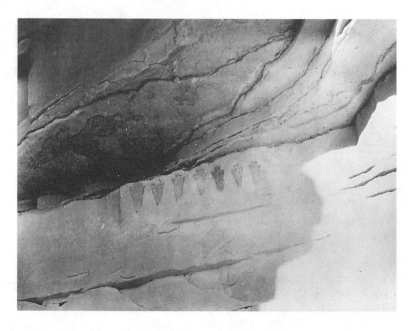

PLATE 22 Plain painted anthropomorphs, Ferron. Beckwith photo.

and later further illustrated and treated in an excellent discussion by Morss (1931, pp. 34–42 and pls. 13–19). Thus it does not need to be described again in detail, and it will suffice merely to review this material and to point out certain aspects of these panels not previously considered.

The files record panels from Capitol Gorge near Fruita and Pleasant Creek, both included in Capitol Reef National Monument. The Fruita petroglyphs are the most striking. As mentioned above, these panels bear certain resemblances to the Vernal district petroglyphs. In the Fruita work the Fremont anthropomorph reigns as the dominant motif among lesser elements (figs. 43–45). He is carved with precision, and here too, an interest in geometric form and the qualities of abstract design are manifest (pl. 24). In particular, the weeping-eye motif occurs again, and headdresses consist of elegantly curved horns. Necklaces may again appear as a complex display of numerous beads or as solid yokes or collars. Lacking here, however, is the highly developed and controlled use of the dot decoration found in Ashley and Dry Fork Valleys, and the variety in all decorative aspects is moderate in comparison. The Fruita figures are often solidly carved and usually have single line arms and splayed fingers. The single feather headdress and the hunched shoulders seem to be char-

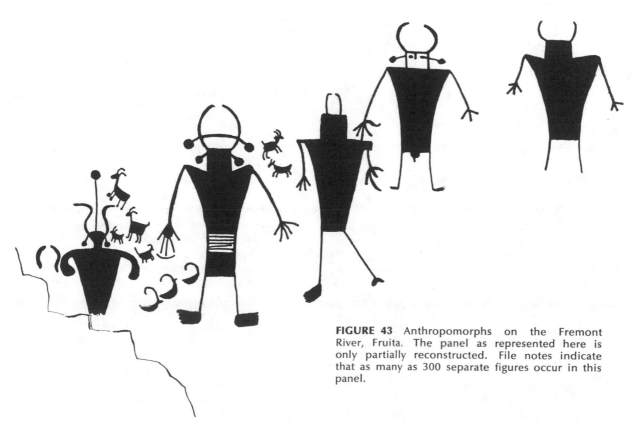

FIGURE 43 Anthropomorphs on the Fremont River, Fruita. The panel as represented here is only partially reconstructed. File notes indicate that as many as 300 separate figures occur in this panel.

FIGURE 44 Single anthropomorph, Fremont River, Fruita. Hunched shoulders and a single feather are characteristic of Fremont representations in this district.

PLATE 24 Incised anthropomorph, Fruita. Figure is deeply incised in wide lines. Compare torso spiral with that in fig. 11 from the Vernal district.

acteristic of the Fremont River locale (fig. 44). Among the subsidiary figures are quadrupeds, wavy and wandering lines, and the characteristic spiral. The mountain sheep are well defined with more or less rectangular or crescent-shaped bodies, again manifesting the Fruita artists' interest in decorative effect. In figure 45, sheep are depicted with raised front feet, which makes them appear playful.

Other petroglyph panels of similar anthropomorphs from Pleasant Creek and Capitol Wash Gorge lack the precision and detail just described (fig. 46, pl. 25). In a small cave in Spring Canyon off Temple Creek south of Fruita, FI–16–2, Morss Site 8 (fig. 47), there is a series of Fremont anthropomorphs approximately one foot high painted in white with red and a trace of yellow trim. All have headgear drawn as vertical lines above the crown and one figure is horned. A second shows a necklace and waist markings. Three of the figures have tiny arms. At Fish Creek Cove, Morss Site 11, a Fremont habitation cave near Grover, Utah, two highly abstract and neatly painted human figures appear beside a shield (pl. 26). These figures are armless and are shown with hunched shoulders. The diagonal torso line characteristic of the southern San Rafael and waist markings can be seen on one anthropomorph. At this site, numerous other Fremont anthropomorphs with elaborate necklaces and headdresses are pecked below, but are in rather poor condition.

The painted shield just referred to, and a series of painted acephalous animals in the same cave which are discussed below, page 60, have precipitated a certain degree of controversy as to their dating. Morss' original opinion (1931, p. 38) was that the shield representation is comparatively recent, this view being based partly on the fresh appearance of the paint, partly on his assignment of a recent date to the actual shields found by Bishop Pectol in a cache near Torrey which resemble modern Athabaskan shields, and partly on the occurrence of shield-shaped paintings in Arizona associated with paintings of European animals. He was "reluctant even to express an opinion as to the age of the large animals."

Later Wormington, pointing to the many shields and shield-bearing figures found in the rock art of the Fremont culture, thought it highly probable that both the shield painting at Fish Creek Cove and the actual Pectol shields were of Fremont origin (1955, pp. 156–157). Aikens, assuming that the Pectol shields are Fremont, has cited them as evidence for Fremont-Athabaskan connections (1967b, p. 201). The Pectol shields (now in the museum at the office of Capitol Reef National Monument) have, however, recently been dated by the C-14 laboratory at U.C.L.A. as "between A.D. 1650 and 1750" (Grant 1967, p. 65), thus confirming Morss' view as to their comparative recency and eliminating them as Fremont culture artifacts unless, indeed, that term is applied to a period centuries later than most authorities would admit.

Morss' current opinion (personal communication), arrived at in the light of Wormington's argument and after reexamining the painting in 1966, is that 1) the Fish Creek shield and acephalous animals are almost certainly contemporary, and 2) they are probably Fremont paintings several centuries older than the Pectol shields, although the possibility of a later date cannot be wholly ruled out. I, likewise, am inclined to accept Wormington's arguments in favor of a Fremont date for the shield paintings. The whole question of the absolute age of the shield motif in the Fremont area and its age relative to that of the motif in the

PLATE 25 Petroglyph of Fremont anthropomorphs, Capitol Wash Gorge. Beckwith photo.

FIGURE 45 Petroglyphs, Fruita.

FIGURE 46 Petroglyphs on Pleasant Creek, Site 5, Image Cave, south of Fruita.

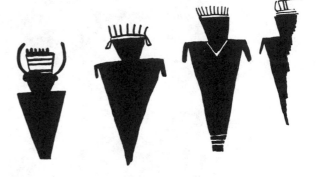

FIGURE 47 Painted anthropomorphs, Spring Canyon, off Temple Creek, south of Fruita, FL–16–2, Morss Site 8.

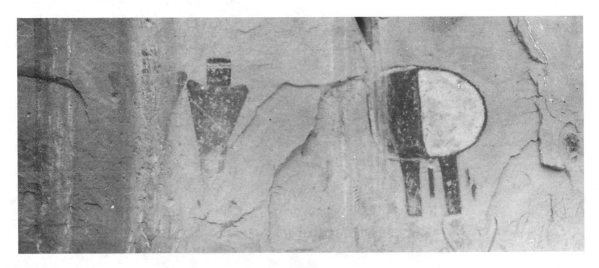

PLATE 26 Painted anthropomorphs and shield, Fish Creek Cove, Morss Site 11, near Grover.

Plains and elsewhere is treated further in connection with the relationships between the rock art of the Fremont and the northern Plains (pp. 142–144).

TEMPLE MOUNTAIN WASH
(42Em65)

Six miles west of Utah Highway 24 at the mouth of Temple Mountain Wash in the San Rafael reef are paintings of Fremont and Barrier Canyon Style origin. One of the two Fremont figures here is a vividly painted anthropomorph with short horns and a thin line extending diagonally across the torso (fig. 48). Encountered here for the first time is the depiction of a low, curved chin. This method of chin representation occurs sporadically among Fremont figures in the southern San Rafael zone. The other figure of Fremont origin is a heroic broad-shouldered anthropomorphic form superimposed on the Barrier Canyon Style paintings (see fig. 71, below).

FIGURE 48 Painted Fremont anthropomorph, Temple Mountain Wash (42Em65), Source: De-Harport photo.

BARRIER (HORSESHOE) CANYON

The majority of Barrier Canyon rock art sites consist of large panels of paintings of the Barrier Canyon Style which are distinguished herein from Fremont rock art and separately treated (pp. 65–83). However, at Horseshoe Rock shelter (SR–12–5) a single panel of painted figures consisting of a long row of painted dots and bulky animals being hunted by a small figure with bow and arrow may be of Fremont origin (fig. 49).

A second site about a mile above the Great Gallery, illustrated by Gunnerson (1969, fig. 31a), is more typically Fremont. The panel consists of scratched anthropomorphs which alternate with painted ones. The figures have bucket heads and headdresses consisting of a series of short lines across the flat crown. Slit eyes are situated high

in the face. Kilts, necklaces, and waistbands are indicated. Over the heads of the figures are two arcs.

THE VICINITY OF THE COLORADO RIVER BETWEEN THE MOUTH OF THE DIRTY DEVIL AND TICABOO CREEK

A few sites have been documented from Ticaboo and Trachyte Creeks and from North Wash (Crescent Creek) and from the mouth of the Dirty Devil River. On the left bank of the Colorado River, Fremont paintings and carvings have been recorded from the mouth of White Canyon. Figures from a number of these sites have been described in previous publications.

At the mouth of the Dirty Devil River, before their inundation by Lake Powell, were five painted designs, four of which were arranged in pairs (fig. 50). These figures were first illustrated in 1877 by Dellenbaugh, who completely misinterpreted them as hieroglyphics, or battle diagrams. It is evident, however, that these figures represent anthropomorphic torsos with the use of highly abstract and geometric forms. The degree of abstraction seen here is again reminiscent of the Uinta region. They also, however, resemble Basketmaker anthropomorphs from Snake Gulch, south of Kanab, Utah.

Typologically more closely related to the figures of the Ashley and Dry Fork Valleys of the Uinta region were a number of shields and shield men at the mouth of White Canyon, now also lost beneath the water (fig. 51). These petroglyphs were discussed by Steward (1941) and were later illustrated again by Wormington (1955, fig. 64 d–l and fig. 65 a–i). (Note: in Wormington's preceding illustration [fig. 63] letters e–h are mislabeled as to provenience. These figures are from the Ashley and Dry Fork Valleys near Vernal (see pl. 2, this paper.) The decorative geometric quality of these shield bearers and the simple abstract designs on the shields are highly reminiscent of the Classic Vernal Style figure. A similar likeness can also be seen in the plain rectangular horned head. The horizontal line between the eyes and month, however, and the orientation of the feet in the same direction are characteristics specific to this vicinity. A similar stylistic quality is also seen in the nearby group on the Colorado River of unelaborated large trapezoidal anthropomorphs depicted with rectangular heads and a diagonal torso stripe (Mallery 1893, fig. 87).

Fremont anthropomorphs without elaborations or other distinctive features are recorded in the

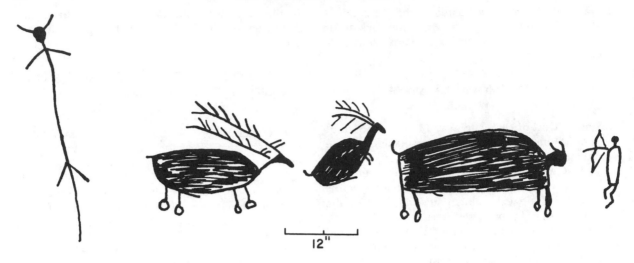

FIGURE 49   Fremont paintings in Horseshoe Rockshelter (SR–12–5), Barrier Canyon.

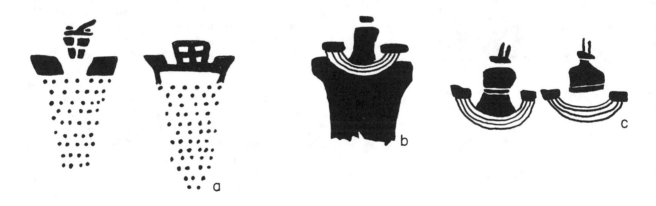

FIGURE 50   Abbreviated anthropomorphic painted figures, mouth of the Dirty Devil River. Source: Dellenbaugh 1877, pp. 174–175.

Scott files from North Wash and Trachyte Canyon. Other Fremont panels have been documented from near the mouth of Trachyte Canyon by Foster (1954, figs. 2 and 3). These panels include similar large undecorated anthropomorphic figures as well as wavy lines and miscellaneous abstract elements. Still farther south at Ticaboo Creek is another site displaying elements characteristic of Fremont work. Included among these figures is a relatively large shield or circular design with sawtooth decoration (Foster 1954, fig. 5).

SALT AND INDIAN CREEKS

Along Salt and Indian Creeks, left bank tributaries to the Colorado in Canyonlands National Park, are a number of paintings and carvings done in the Fremont style. Oddly enough, however, the Fremont style rock paintings and carvings from this region, such as those at LS–14–11 (42Sa1563) described below, are found in consistent association with Mesa Verde architectural remains and habitation refuse, including pottery (Gunnerson 1969,

p. 45 and Sharrock 1966b, pp. 61–62 and 66–67). It is Sharrock's opinion that the Fremont motifs were borrowed wholesale by the late Pueblo II and early Pueblo III Mesa Verde occupants without an immigration of Fremont people, since all habitation sites yielded purely Mesa Verde material. For further discussion concerning the authorship of these paintings see page 148 of this paper.

Some of the representations of large Fremont anthropomorphs from these drainages are basically quite simple (figs. 52–54). Only heads and torsos without appendages are portrayed. At Salt Creek site LS–14–11, painted anthropomorphic figures occurring singly or in pairs display the extended chin described above (fig. 52). Torso decoration is rendered by means of vertical lines convergent at the waist or in one instance a single diagonal line such as was present in the Temple Mountain Wash and Fish Creek Cove examples. Necklaces and possible shoulder bobs also occur at this site. Facial decoration or masks are represented and one pair of figures displays slit eyes high in the face.

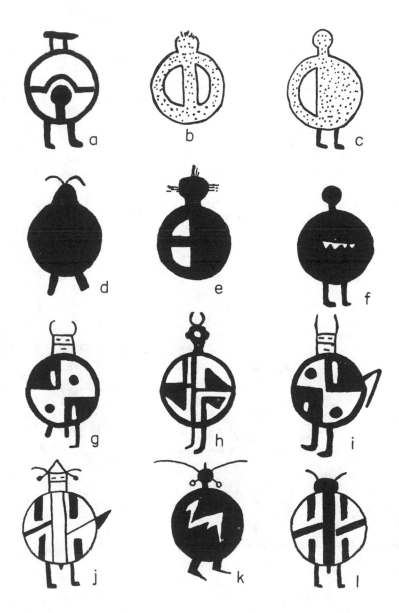

FIGURE 51 Shield-bearing figures from the mouth of White Canyon. Source: Wormington 1955, figs. 64, d-1 and 65, a–c.

FIGURE 52 Painted anthropomorphs, Salt Creek Canyon (LS–14–11; also 42Sa1563).

At another site on Indian Creek, LS–14–3, pecked or scratched and possibly painted unelaborated anthropomorphic forms occur in association with large circular objects perhaps representing shields (fig. 53). Serpents and fat mountain sheep (not illustrated) are also depicted here. Other elements occurring in Salt Creek panels are ladders (Pierson 1962, p. 3), sawtooth designs, zigzags, bisected circles, and spirals (fig. 54). Large shield bearers are also present at 42Sa1506 at the Peephole Spring site (fig. 55).

One panel in the Salt Creek drainage (42Sa1629) is worthy of detailed consideration. It consists of four elaborately painted anthropomorphs (pl. 27). These complex figures may be the same as those described by Pierson (1962, p. 2) as having elaborate face masks of a type peculiar to the Needles area, and as being greater than life size and painted in red and white. Although clearly related to the usual Fremont anthropomorph, these particular figures stand in marked contrast. The stiff trapezoidal body is lost, and instead they are dumpy short-waisted beings with heavy, large rounded chins. Their torsos are decorated with the convergent vertical lines seen in other Salt Creek paintings, and in addition sashes and some suggestion of kilts are present. Necklaces consist of a string with a single center bead. The eyes are depicted as a slit alone or within an oval, the latter device resembling the "coffee bean" eye of certain Fremont figurines (Morss 1931, pls. 26 c and 27 c). The tops of the heads are flat and on either side of the face there appears a shoulder bob. The unusualness of these four anthropomorphs is seen not only in their expressive contrast with the ordinary Fremont figure, but in their specific resemblances to Fremont figurines. As pointed out above, this relationship is shared by other southern San Rafael representations, particularly in the Salt Creek drainage.

Other paintings of similar complexity from Salt Creek are on record in Anthropology Department files at the University of Utah in Salt Lake City.

MOAB AND THE LA SAL MOUNTAINS

Other Fremont rock art sites near the Colorado River have been recorded from the vicinity of Moab. Some of these sites have been illustrated previously by Steward (1929, pl. 83). Steward's photographs show no large Fremont anthropomorphs, but instead, panels of small solidly

FIGURE 53 Anthropomorphic forms, Indian Creek (LS–14–3). Figures appear to be defined by scratching, although some painting is also possible.

FIGURE 54 Petroglyphs, Indian Creek. Source: Charles B. Boogher photo.

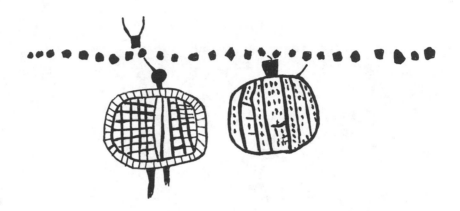

FIGURE 55 Painted shield bearers (42Sa1506) Salt Creek. Source: Charles B. Boogher photo.

pecked figures which in general style and content are much like those of the northern San Rafael zone. Many of the figures are crudely executed and ill-defined (figs. 56 and 57). Somewhat unusual are the numerous handprints, some of which are attached to long lines, and the bearlike tracks, the latter being a popular motif in western Colorado sites. Other sites in the area display similar figures and horned variations of the Fremont anthropomorph (fig. 58). Finally, the Potash Road petroglyph site (not illustrated) is characterized by southern San Rafael type anthropomorphs with round hairbobs. The panel in general, although clearly of Fremont origin, bears aesthetic likeness to Anasazi work.

East of Moab and the Colorado River, numerous Fremont and Anasazi rock art sites have been recorded in the La Sal Mountains (Hunt 1953, figs. 75, 76, 83–86). Unlike the Canyonlands situation, architecture and habitation refuse, including pottery and basketry, bore Fremont as well as

Anasazi resemblances (Hunt 1953). The Fremont petroglyphs are reproduced by Hunt as isolated figures, so that it is impossible to understand the total context from which they derive. Illustrated are examples of horned trapezoidal figures and men with helmetlike headdresses and elk antlers, reminiscent of those from Sieber Canyon (see p. 27) and the Classic Vernal Style variant described on page 15. In addition, Hunt records numerous mountain sheep and abstract designs, and to the latter she ascribes a Great Basin likeness (1953, p. 179). These figures include the usual spirals, wavy lines, dot rows, ladders, and various circle motifs encountered in other Fremont sites. The Anasazi occupation of the region is evidenced in the rock art by rows of hand-holding figures, flute players, and animal tracks.

The northern as well as southern affiliations of the Fremont rock art of the Moab-La Sal district indicate that this is an area of mixed influences within the Fremont configuration (see p. 28).

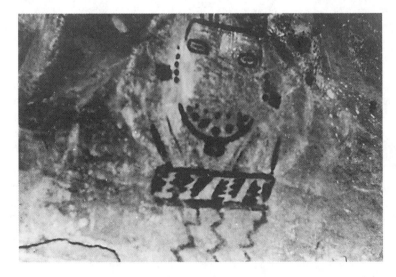

PLATE 27 Painted anthropomorphs, Salt Creek Canyon. Note the negative hand-prints over which these paintings are superimposed. Charles B. Boogher photos.

FIGURE 56 Petroglyphs, Moab. Source: Steward 1929, pl. 83 a.

THE SOUTHERN PERIPHERY

Finally, a small number of Fremont rock paintings and petroglyphs have been recorded from the country to the northwest of the Colorado River south of the Dirty Devil, constituting the lower end of the southern San Rafael rock art zone. Most of the data available from this fringe area derive from the scattered published references of previous investigators.

Just as upstream on the opposite bank of the Colorado in the Canyonlands area there is evidence of contact between the Fremont and the Mesa Verde Anasazi, so it has been demonstrated that the present area was a zone of contact between the Fremont and Kayenta Puebloan peoples. Here there was a greater degree of interdigitation of the two occupations and more mixture of ceramics or other diagnostic artifacts at particular sites, although the evidence does not support any substantial degree of blending of the two cultures. Parts of the Escalante drainage show a heavy Kayenta occupation and favorable spots in the higher elevations, such as the Kaiparowitz Plateau and Boulder Valley at the northern edge of the Aquarius Plateau, attracted a large Kayenta population for around 150 years in Pueblo II and early Pueblo III. Elsewhere, however, the uplands were predominantly Fremont, as was Harris Wash in the Escalante drainage, where all sites yielded Turner Gray sherds, figurines, moccasins, and other Fremont traits. In addition, the Glen Canyon right bank survey found Fremont sherds, other artifacts, and storage chambers scattered at lower elevations near the Colorado from the dam site below Waheap Creek up the river into the Fremont domi-

nated territory at the mouth of the Dirty Devil (R. Lister 1959a, Suhm 1959, Lister and Lister 1961, F. C. Lister 1964; see particularly the latter's distribution map, fig. 1). The Fremont occupation of Harris Wash and the probable Fremont use of the Escalante Valley as a corridor of movement and communication with Pueblo groups to the south sufficiently explain the concentration of Fremont rock art sites found throughout the length of the Escalante and in nearby locales such as the tip of the Kaiparowitz Plateau and the mouth of Rock Creek Canyon, and make it unnecessary to postulate any wholesale adoption of Fremont styles by Puebloan artists. In another study, based on the distribution of Fremont ware and sherds of the Tsegi series in the Waterpocket Fold, Lister singles out the east flank of this valley as another corridor of movement and cultural contact between the Fremont and the Anasazi (1959b, p. 302). No Fremont rock art sites, however, have been documented from this drainage.

Most of the recorded Fremont sites from this region are located north of the Colorado and west of the Escalante River (fig. 2). One exception to this distribution is a rock painting ambiguously located on the San Juan River somewhere between its junction with the Colorado and the mouth of Oljeto Wash. This panel displays painted representations of trapezoidal anthropomorphic figures. One is depicted with a tapered waist and carries a small shield with concentric circle decoration (fig. 59).

A number of Fremont rock art sites have been recorded from western tributaries of the Escalante. At the mouth of this river at Site NA 5368 there are painted anthropomorphs with horned and helmet headgear. Other anthropomorphs at this site are carved abbreviated representations of heads and torsos alone. Further description of these figures may be found in Foster (1954, p. 14 and fig. 10) and Fowler (1959b, p. 39).

About five miles from the mouth of the Escalante in Davis Gulch there is a striking Fremont panel of white paintings (42Ka235) briefly described in earlier publications by Lister (1959a, p. 104 and fig. 31) and Gunnerson (1959b, p. 149). At this site a dozen or so anthropomorphs occur in conjunction with various circular motifs probably representing shields (pl. 28). At first glance the anthropomorphs appear to be highly abbreviated, but fainter paint traces visible in the photographs suggest that two types of paint were used originally and that one of them has been largely eroded away, and as a result some of the original figure delineation has been lost. The anthropomorphs display trapezoidal torsos with a wide variety of decorative patterns. Necklaces are of the solid yoke variety. The head, which in some cases has been obscured, is generally rectangular and horned headgear is depicted. Several figures hold shields at arm's length. All but one of these circular devices is decorated with geometric designs. The exception displays the negative image of a Fremont anthropomorph.

From farther up the Escalante in Coyote Gulch, Lister (1959a, p. 134) describes but does not illustrate life-size human figures with headdresses at 42Ka225. In addition, at 42Ka172 in Dry Fork of Coyote Gulch, there are petroglyphs of anthropomorphs which more closely resemble figure types found in western Utah (fig. 60). The anthropomorphs are highly abstracted and simplified. Distinctive are the broad triangular body form and the large heads bearing no features or other elaborations. Spirals and concentric circles are described as associated (Lister 1959a, p. 122). The occurrence in Coyote Gulch of Sevier type anthropomorphs, suggesting contact with the west, is supported by the presence at many Escalante drainage sites of Snake Valley Gray and Snake Valley Black-on-Gray pottery (Gunnerson 1959b, p. 15).

In addition to these anthropomorphic figures of Fremont type, Suhm (1959, p. 278, fig. 18) and Fowler (1963, p. 37) report paintings from Harris Wash at sites 42Ga276 and 42Ga288 which may also be Fremont handiwork. The paintings consist of geometric elements of straight and zigzag lines and a row of solid triangles. Similar motifs are frequently encountered in Fremont sites farther north, and because this wash, and specifically the latter site, 42Ga288, yielded evidence of a strong

FIGURE 57 Petroglyphs, Moab. Source: Steward 1929, pl. 83 b.

Fremont occupation, it is reasonable to suppose that the paintings are of Fremont origin. Fowler (1963, fig. 17) also illustrates from the Fremont site of Circle Terrace, 42Ga286, a panel of quadrupeds and anthropomorphs and two large trapezoidal outline forms.

West of the Escalante drainage a red, helmeted figure carrying a small shield is painted at an unnumbered site on the southeastern edge of the Kaiparowitz Plateau (fig. 61). At Rock Creek, a single painting of a human figure with trapezoidal torso and yoke type collar, associated with an ex-

tensive campsite of indeterminate nature, has been reported by Lister (1958, p. 15).

Two sites have been recorded from northern Arizona in which large Fremont-like horned anthropomorphs are depicted. One of these sites, located south of Kanab, Utah, near the Vermillion Cliffs, displays neatly carved large trapezoidal men with horned, bucket-shaped heads (fig. 62). The second site, near Winslow illustrated by Steward (1929, pl. 84b) consists of elaborate figures with highly decorative torso patterning. These latter figures are viewed by Grant (1968, p. 123) as being akin to Coso Range motifs in southern California.

FIGURE 58 Petroglyphs, Moab. Source: Colorado Museum of Natural History photo.

FIGURE 59 Painted anthropomorph holding shield, San Juan River "probably between mouth and Moonlight Creek" (field notes). NA2699. Source: Rainbow Bridge-Monument Valley Expedition photo.

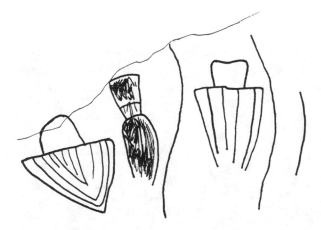

FIGURE 60 Petroglyphs, Dry Fork, Coyote Gulch, 42Ka172. Source: photo courtesy of David S. Dibble.

FIGURE 61 Red painted anthropomorph with helmet and shield. Anthropomorph is four feet tall. South edge of the Kaiparowitz Plateau. Source: C. Sharp photo.

FIGURE 62   Fremont type petroglyphs on the Vermillion Cliffs, south of Kanab.

PLATE 28 White paintings of Fremont anthropomorphs and shields, Davis Gulch, Escalante drainage.
Photos courtesy of David S. Dibble.

III

Specialized Developments in the
Eastern Fremont Area

Before we consider the Fremont rock art of western Utah, which participates in varying degrees in the basic Fremont stylistic configuration seen in the eastern area, it is necessary to describe minor specialized Fremont developments and other stylistic manifestations also occurring within the geographic area of the eastern Fremont culture.

SMALL HUMPBACK ANTHROPOMORPHS

The various small and informal anthropomorphic figures that occur in Fremont contexts have been discussed with the bulk of the Fremont material. There is another type of figure, however, that appears sporadically throughout the San Rafael region. This figure is small and thin and is usually shown with a large hump or device which may represent a carrying basket (Morss 1970, personal communication). These anthropomorphs commonly have long legs and arms and are quite graceful and delicately rendered. They usually carry staffs and may appear in contexts apart from other Fremont work. Sites with these figures have been recorded from Fruita (Morss 1931, pl. 16), Nine Mile Canyon (Reagan 1932, p. 41), Temple Creek Canyon (Steward 1929, fig. 85) and on Dry Wash (42Em68) (figs. 63 and 64). It is possible that they represent a particular personage of Fremont mythology.

BLACK BOULDER PETROGLYPHS

Abstract designs and serpents pecked on black boulders are reported from the southern San Rafael (Morss 1931, pp. 15 and 34, and Gunnerson 1957, fig. 25). These petroglyphs seem to be associated with rock circle sites, and according to Morss are always on a hillside facing down and away from the houses. The subjects depicted are invariably serpents, spirals, or mazes. More sites of this nature are needed to determine whether or not the black boulder figures might be an eastern manifestation of the Great Basin Curvilinear Style.

THE PAINTED ANIMALS AT FISH CREEK COVE, SITE 11

The group of painted animals in a shelter at Fish Creek Cove near Grover remains an anomaly (fig. 65). The nearly life-sized animals are painted in red with an unparalleled skill in a surprisingly naturalistic style. Although some tend to have an oval body form, the grace with which the line of the neck, withers, and backs are rendered with an accenting heavy line is reminiscent of Old World cave paintings. Another unusual aspect to these animals is that, with one exception, they lack faces or heads. Circles and small quadrupeds are painted over and near the large animals and Fremont type figures are carved over other paintings.

Other acephalous animals have been noted at Site 31 in Nine Mile Canyon, a rock shelter which contained both Basketmaker and Fremont materials, and in association with a painted Barrier Canyon Style anthropomorph on North Wash (pl. 18). Similar animals of heroic size, but not lacking heads, are painted below and appear to be contemporary with the Barrier Canyon Style anthropomorphs at Temple Mountain Wash (42Em 65). Although Morss has expressed another viewpoint (see p. 47), it may be suggested on the basis of the superimpositions and of the new evidence at Temple Mountain Wash that the Fish Creek Cove animals were executed by Barrier Canyon Style artists. As such, they may have preceded in time the Fremont work also present in this shelter.

See chapter VII for a discussion of the dating of the Barrier Canyon Style.

MUDDY RIVER AND
ROCHESTER CREEK JUNCTION
FL–4–1

South of Ferron on a rocky prominence overlooking the junction of Rochester Creek and the Muddy River, a petroglyph panel is carved on a large boulder (pl. 29 and fig. 66). Part of this panel has been recently illustrated by Gunnerson (1969, fig. 25b). It is unlike other petroglyphs encountered in this study. The panel is busy with closely spaced linear and solid elements, and a number of figures are superimposed by a huge arc of parallel lines, one meter high and one meter wide (Gunnerson 1969, p. 78). Many of the anthropomorphs bear a resemblance to Barrier Canyon Style figures in head and body form, in the presence of eyes which are round or "bugged," and in their long, curved antennae. Many figures are pictured in profile and are running, gesturing with their arms, or holding small objects.

The most peculiar elements are the zoomorphic creatures. Among them the usual mountain sheep is rare. Many figures appear to be mythical or supernatural in character, and some of these are portrayed in detail. Two groups of these animals are shown in attitudes of great ferocity. With bared teeth and stiff tails stretched out behind them, held high, or curved over their backs, they are racing toward each other in what promises to be a wild encounter.

There are no parallels between this site and other petroglyph panels represented in the files.

Gunnerson (1969, p. 78) is of the opinion that a number of these creatures, particularly the hippopotamus- and alligatorlike creatures, are of recent derivation. However, field inspection of the site indicated that on the basis of patination and technical execution, these figures are not recent and are an integral part of the original panel.

In the vicinity of the petroglyphs were found apparent open hearths and abundant knapping debris, and the location of the entire complex indicates that it may have been a hunting camp site. The cultural origin of the figures remains somewhat in question.

MISCELLANEOUS PAINTED
ABSTRACT DESIGNS

From the Vernal District and from Chandler Canyon in the northern San Rafael the files illustrate two rock painting sites with abstract designs. The elements consist of short lines in sets of four, three, or two. In one instance, these are bordered by asterisk motifs. These panels closely resemble the Great Basin Painted Style defined by Heizer and Baumhoff (1962, p. 207) although they find counterparts in Fremont elements as well.

From Black Dragon Canyon north of the San Rafael River are paintings which are more complex and stylistically diverse from those discussed above. These figures are painted in red and dark green and the dominant feature is the use of short lines arranged in massed ranks or forming part of a design element (Morss 1931, pp. 41–42 and pl. 19 c and d). Their date is unknown. Morss mentions similar sites in Capital Gorge and in Dry Creek of Nine Mile Canyon.

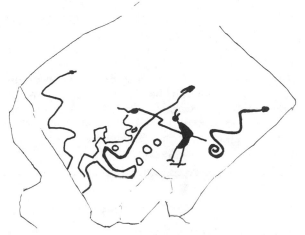

FIGURE 63 Petroglyphs of humpback figures, Nine Mile Canyon. Source: Reagan-Nusbaum photo, Panel NP 10.

FIGURE 64 Petroglyphs with humpback figure, Dry Wash (42Em68). Source: Beckwith photo.

FIGURE 65   Painted animals at Fish Creek Cove, Site 11, Grover. The figures, painted in red, are nearly life-size.

He sums up the site nicely in a single statement: "Taken as a whole, the pictographs at this site seem quite distinct from those at other sites but present familiar details which make it impossible to attribute them with certainty to a separate period or people" (1931, p. 42).

PAINTED HANDPRINTS

On the basis of the file sample, panels of painted handprints are relatively rare in eastern Utah sites outside of the Anasazi area. Sites are recorded from Hill Creek, Oak Creek, and Barrier Canyon. The Hill and Oak Creek panels each consist of a single line of a few solid prints. In Barrier Canyon site, SR–12–3, scattered rows of striped prints occur (pl. 30). Prints of this nature are created by running the fingers of the opposite hand through the paint before the stamped impression with the painted hand is made (Schaafsma 1966b, p. 36).

In four Salt Creek sites on the left bank of the Colorado, masses of solid and striped prints and negative images occur in red, white, and yellow. The proliferation of the handprint motif here and the presence of an associated pottery design motif suggest that these figures may be of Pueblo origin.

Panels of painted handprints are a common phenomenon in Anasazi sites. They are also, however, a widespread theme in Indian rock art in general, and panels of handprints are reported from as far north as central Montana (Conner 1962, p. 25).

SCRATCHED DESIGNS

Were it not for the fact that crude scratching in west central Nevada consisting of straight lines, sun figures, and cross-hatching were placed by Heizer and Baumhoff (1962) into the separate stylistic category of "Great Basin Scratched," similar crude scratched designs faintly visible in certain photographs from the eastern Fremont area would probably have been overlooked.

Scratched designs are visible in only five panels on file although they may occur more frequently in actual fact. These sites are widely scattered in the San Rafael region. At Ferron, large grids of scratched lines occur with a panel of painted anthropomorphs (pl. 23). It is impossible to tell from the photograph whether or not the scratchings are superimposed upon the paintings. That they are contemporary or later is evident from the scratched antlers which appear on one of the figures. In Florence Canyon, an eastern tributary of the Green, and in Bear Canyon of the Price River drainage, scratched designs consist of stepped lines, grids, and sawtooth decoration (pl. 31). In Barrier Canyon at SR–12–4a, scratchings are less rigidly geometric, and plant forms, animals, and vague linear patterns occur.

GLEN CANYON STYLE 5

The Glen Canyon Style 5 was defined by Turner on the basis of his research in that region (1963, pp. 7–8). Other Glen Canyon petroglyphs in that style have been described by Lister (1958, p. 38) and Lipe (1960, p. 73). The style seems to have occurred most frequently in this region, which is peripheral to the area under current study. Oddly enough, however, Style 5 shows up again in the Dry Fork Valley near Vernal (Site 42Un59), in a panel of figures 78 feet long and 12 feet wide (fig. 67).

The large anthropomorphs with bodies defined in crude rectangular outlines and decorated with cross-hatching are typical of this style. These

PLATE 29   Petroglyphs, Rochester Creek and Muddy River Junction. The unusual figures in this panel find few parallels in Utah rock art.

PLATE 30   Painted handprints, in white, red, and orange, SR–12–3, Barrier Canyon.

figures have small heads, and tiny arms extend upward from the shoulders. The elaborate headdresses are also characteristic. Similarly, rectilinear outline forms are present in the animal representations, which also display the insignificant stick limbs and small heads as seen on the anthropomorphic figures. The large rake element is also characteristic of this style.

Research in the Glen Canyon led Turner to conclude that Style 5 persisted in this region no later than A.D. 1050, as it was found associated with early pottery sites as well as with sites at which no pottery was present. No beginning date for the style has been determined. Turner has suggested that it may commence much earlier than the 100 B.C. date that he tentatively proposed in the

FIGURE 66   Petroglyphs at the junction of the Muddy River and Rochester Creek (FL–4–1.).

monograph (Turner 1966, personal communication). The Dry Fork panel is probably not earlier than the advent of horticulture in this area, however, if the depiction of the corn plant is contemporary with the rest of the figures. Nevertheless, the above observations are consistent with Reagan's opinion that the panel consisted of "some of the oldest glyphs in the entire region." (Reagan Notes, MNM files, p. 31).

Why this distinctive style present in Glen Canyon should reappear in northeastern Utah with no sites showing up in the intervening area is hard to explain. It is possible that because of its relatively great age many examples of this style have been obliterated or have been overlooked by the majority of investigators.

THE BARRIER CANYON STYLE

Within the San Rafael Fremont region there is a group of panels of rock paintings in which life-size anthropomorphic forms are dominant, but which are stylistically distinct from the Fremont tradition described above. A concentration of sites occurs in the general vicinity of the confluence of the Green and Colorado Rivers (fig. 68) between Barrier Canyon (also known as Horseshoe Canyon) and North Wash (also known as Crescent Creek). In addition, sites in Buckhorn Wash, Thompson, and Moab are also documented and another site at the junction of Clear and Ivie Creeks is described by Taylor (1957, p. 80, fig. 30). Three panels in the vicinity of Ferron and two more in the Head

PLATE 31   Scratched designs in panel with pecked anthropomorphic figures of unknown origin, Florence Canyon, ET–9–5. Claflin-Emerson Expedition photo.

FIGURE 67 Petroglyphs, Glen Canyon Style 5, Dry Fork Valley (42Un59). Source: Reagan-Nusbaum photo, Panel P 3.

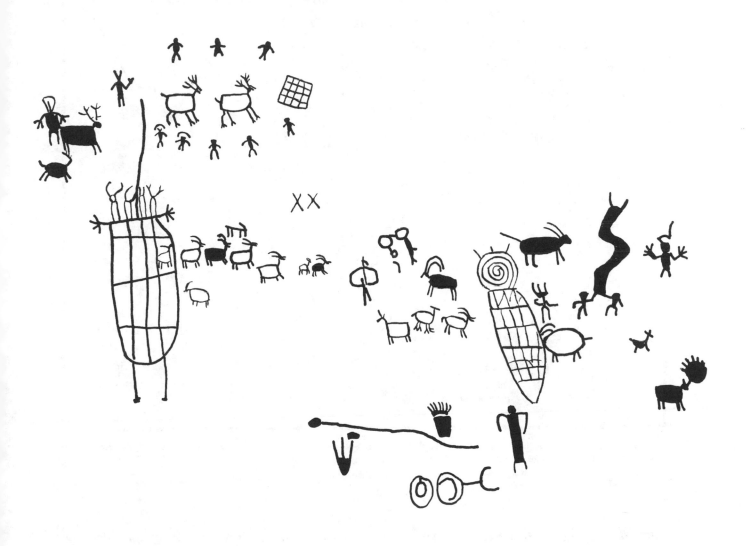

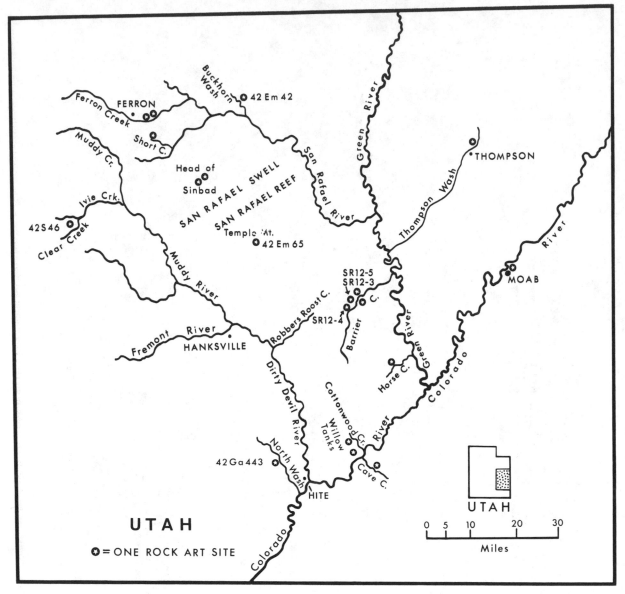

FIGURE 68 Map showing locations of Barrier Canyon Style sites. Each circle represents one site. Note: not all sites have numbers. Site locations are approximate.

of Sinbad, northeast of the San Rafael Knob, were recently observed by the writer. These last sites are noted on the map, but not described herein. The name Barrier Canyon Style has been chosen as an overall designation for these paintings after the tributary of the Green on which the largest number of the striking panels has been recorded.

Problems relating to these paintings will be discussed in another section. They have never been securely dated, and their stylistic relationships seem to be complex. This is an opportune moment to describe the style in some detail, since these sites have heretofore been mentioned only briefly in the published literature (Morss 1931, pp. 38–40; Beckwith 1934; Steward 1941, pl. 52 a; Gunnerson 1957, p. 145, and 1969, figs. 26–30; Taylor 1957, p. 80; Lister 1959a, p. 121, and Grant 1967, pp. 116–117).

The elements of this style and their various attributes are summarized in table 4.* The dominant motif in these paintings is the long dark form of the human torso which appears in every Barrier Canyon Style site and constitutes 79 percent of all the elements present in a total inventory of the Barrier Canyon Style elements (fig. 7). No distinction is made in table 4 between the large anthropomorphic figures and the few small ones that occur since, with few exceptions, they are typologically the same. These highly abstracted and mummylike anthropomorphs which seem to hover against the cliff walls determine the overall aesthetic impact of the Barrier Canyon Style, not only because of their repeated occurrence in each site, but also because of their great size in comparison with the few other elements occurring with them which are often tiny adjuncts to the major anthropomorphic theme.

The human forms vary from sketchily painted shapes to precisely painted figures which exhibit a high degree of detailed decoration (compare, for instance, plates 33 and 37). The characteristic body type is long and tapering. Long rectangular and broader triangular forms are also seen in small proportions. An occasional anthropomorph at the Great Gallery in Barrier Canyon has sloping shoulders and is bottlelike in basic configuration (pls. 35 and 36); in other instances the shoulders are rounded and protruding and in a few extreme cases are extended into rudimentary arms (figs. 69 a and 72 b). Many anthropomorphs are depicted without arms or legs, but arms and legs may be present, particularly in special instances in which a figure is carrying something or taking part in some activity.

The treatment of the head is also varied. At one Barrier Canyon Site (SR–12–5) heads are lacking altogether on some figures, while others have small round heads and long necks (fig. 72 a and b). In other sites, the heads of these anthropomorphs are large and round, often flattened on top, or angular and bucket-shaped. Facial features, present in Thompson, Moab, and Great Gallery panels, are in the form of round staring eyes which lend to these beings a very ghostlike appearance, an effect which is accentuated by their frequent lack of appendages. A bug-eyed figure is present in the Temple Mountain Wash group, a feature also found in Barrier Canyon Style anthropomorphs in the Sinbad and Ferron districts.

* Note: This table was made on the basis of the photographs. Additional figures observed in the field just before the manuscript was written are included in the text description, but were not added to the tables.

Decorative detail is distinctive. Certain forms of headgear occur repeatedly, although the majority of figures lack this attribute. Short antennalike projections consisting of paired sets of two or three thin lines at either side of the top of the head appear most consistently (fig. 70). Straight lines vaguely resembling rabbit ears and outward curving devices like horns or long antennae are also portrayed on occasion. Other Barrier Canyon Style anthropomorphs wear a white crown of dots or short lines (pl. 38 and fig. 77). The decorative treatment of the torso may be intricate and textilelike, although most figures are simply plain. The use of white dots in various linear patterns is the most highly preferred mode of torso ornamentation, although vertical stripes and zigzags or a combination of these elements with fine incised lines may produce the textilelike effect mentioned above. At times, the decoration is arranged in horizontal bands to complicate the complexity of the design. One large Great Gallery anthropomorph has animals painted in the chest region (fig. 73). Simpler torso embellishment consists of heavier vertical striping of the entire figure, or of the presence of an open panel of striped decoration in the midst of a solidly painted field (fig. 72 b). A number of figures are flanked with zigzag lines or other simple motifs, and a few carry wild plants or other objects, as described below.

Aside from the zigzags and other motifs flanking certain large anthropomorphic figures, abstract elements are almost entirely lacking in panels of this style. Naturalistic renderings of animal or bird figures, however, are visible in association with the anthropomorphs in over half of the Barrier Canyon Style panels. Field observations indicate that this occurrence is actually higher, as such figures, which are often tiny, were partially obscured by the effects of photography. Finally, there is the large companion quadruped, probably a dog, with its tail curled over its back (pl. 38, figs. 71 and 75). It is worthy of note that the small figures do not occur at random as in Fremont rock art, but are arranged in composed groups or are directly associated with the large anthropomorphs.

Since these minor elements, as well as other aspects of the Barrier Canyon Style paintings, are of considerable interest, sites merit description on an individual basis.

Buckhorn Wash, 42Em42. On the north side of Buckhorn Wash, about four miles above its confluence with the San Rafael River, is an extensive panel displaying a number of unusual features. The

PLATE 32 Barrier Canyon Style paintings, Moab. The shields are superimposed over some of the anthropomorphs, and thus appear to be more recent. Beckwith photo.

site is mentioned briefly by Gunnerson in connection with his survey of this area (1957, p. 145). The paintings have been heavily defaced. The panel, 100 feet long, consists of a series of elongated life-size anthropomorphs painted in red, several of which are holding snakes, rakes, and other objects (fig. 69 a and b). Also present are three arcs similar to those seen in several Fremont sites. Additional elements are a fringed oval object and a small vertical animal resembling the squirrel pouches in Navajo sandpaintings. Also present but not illustrated is an anthropomorph being attacked by a coiled rattlesnake.

Of special interest here is a series of smaller, highly attenuated anthropomorphs painted over an arc above the main group (fig. 69 b). These figures

hold oval and bell-shaped objects unidentifiable in the photograph. A visit to the site showed that some of the figures have small quadrupeds painted above their heads or are approached by birds (not illustrated). Long wavy lines, stripes, and a possible serpent accentuate the vertical emphasis of this composition.

Thompson Wash, 42Gr274–277. North of Thompson is an extensive site consisting of several panels and rock art of various origins. The Fremont figures at this site were discussed earlier. In the main panel of Barrier Canyon Style paintings, nineteen major anthropomorphs are depicted, of which four are pictured here (fig. 70). The ghostlike visage of the Thompson figures was mentioned above in the

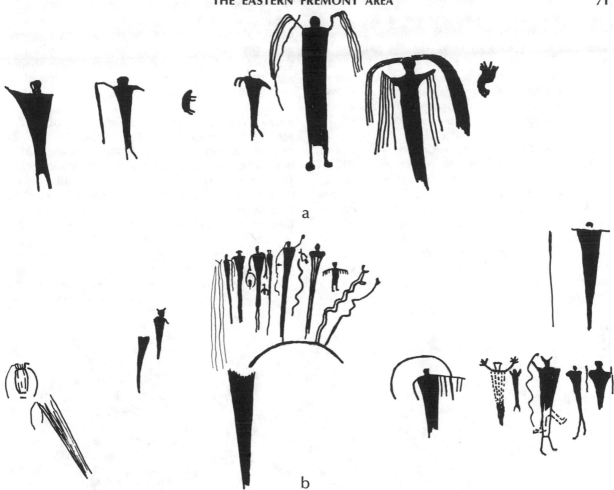

a

b

FIGURE 69 Buckhorn Wash paintings, Barrier Canyon Style (42Em42). A partial reconstruction. a, left-hand side as face panel; b, right-hand side as face panel. Note that in 'b' the third figure from the right was originally painted as indicated by the solid line. Source: Beckwith photos.

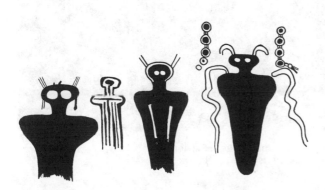

FIGURE 70 Barrier Canyon Style paintings, Thompson Wash. Only four out of nineteen figures present are illustrated here.

general discussion. Small deer are painted on the shoulders of one anthropomorph and ten more are depicted at the side of another. The painting of a scorpion is also present at this site. Snakes occur either separately or held by the anthropomorphs.

Petroglyphs have been subsequently carved over some of the paintings and sandal prints are carved on the horizontal rock faces below the paintings.

Junction of Clear and Ivie Creeks, 42Sv6. This panel, described previously by Taylor (1957, p. 80) consists primarily of seven anthropomorphic forms painted in a red-brown color, and all are considerably faded. Six of these forms are arranged in groups around a single central large anthropomorph which is quite plain except for the presence of antennae headgear. The head of this figure is also flanked on either side by a circle-dot motif. A large set of concentric circles painted in bright red also occurs below this group. The

bright color of this design and its absence in other Barrier Canyon Style paintings make its contemporaneity with the other figures questionable. Fremont cultural remains were found in the shelter and paintings of Fremont origin were found in another shelter in the vicinity.

Moab. The Moab panel has been previously described by Beckwith (1934, p. 177). The figures here are defined in pecked outlines and are further decorated with red and white painting (pl. 32). The long tapered body, the antennalike headdresses, and the staring eyes are characteristic features of Barrier Canyon Style figures elsewhere. One or two figures hold snakes. Other anthropomorphs are approached by small deer, not visible in the illustration. Of special interest here are the large shields held by certain figures. A visit to this site indicated that the shields, although apparently of some antiquity, have been superimposed over

PLATE 33 Barrier Canyon Style paintings, Barrier Canyon, SR–12–3. Very little detail is present in this group.

FIGURE 71 Barrier Canyon Style figures at Temple Mountain Wash (42Em65). The large, broad-shouldered figure is believed to be of Fremont origin. It is superimposed over a bug-eyed Barrier Canyon Style anthropomorph. The Barrier Canyon Style figures are more faded and the large animals at the base of the line of anthropomorphs have been broken off. Source: DeHarport photo.

some of the Barrier Canyon Style figures. Whether or not this was done by the Barrier Canyon Style artists themselves or later comers to the site is impossible to tell.

Petroglyphs are carved over the paintings at this site and sandal prints are carved in the horizontal rock below the paintings, as at Thompson Wash.

Temple Mountain Wash, 42Em65. The Fremont paintings present at this site, one of which is superimposed on the Barrier Canyon Style panel, have been discussed earlier.

The six large Barrier Canyon Style figures are somewhat faded and duller in color than the paintings in the Fremont tradition. The largest Barrier Canyon Style figure has white dot decoration over the red torso and holds a large snake (fig. 71). To the right of this figure the Fremont painting is superimposed over a bug-eyed anthropomorph in the Barrier Canyon Style. Wavy lines flank other Barrier Canyon Style anthropomorphs, and another figure (not illustrated) has four tiny dogs next to it (Dean Brimhall 1970, personal communication).

The large companion dog in this panel is painted with a hairy tail. Beneath the main panel the cliff has broken off, but remaining are the top portions of the backs and heads of what appear to be two unusually large quadrupeds similar to those painted at Fish Creek Cove.

Barrier (Horseshoe) Canyon. At site SR–12–3 (pl. 33) and one site lacking numbered identification in Barrier Canyon, very little detail is present in addition to the long simple forms of the anthropomorphic figures. Figures at SR–12–3 are painted in red mud rather than with the usual mineral pigment (Gunnerson 1957, p. 65). Detail that does occur in SR–12–3 is listed in table 4. The paintings at SR–12–5 (Horseshoe Rock Shelter) are also done with mud, but in this case care was taken to execute the figures in contrasting shades for a pleasing effect. Also much more attention was given to detail in this panel (fig. 72). Form variations occurring at Horseshoe Rock Shelter were mentioned in the general discussion. The results of excavations carried out in the habitation refuse of this

a

b

FIGURE 72 Mud paintings at Horseshoe Rock Shelter (SR–12–5), Barrier Canyon. a, left half as face panel; b, right half as face panel.

FIGURE 73 Great Gallery ghost figures (SR–12–4), Barrier Canyon. These life-size figures are notable for their intricate body decoration. Source: Grant 1967 p. 114 ff., and Scott file photo.

rock shelter are summarized from Gunnerson (1969, pp. 67–68) on page 128 of this paper.

The Great Gallery, SR-12-4. The long wall of a rock shelter painted with extraordinarily detailed life-sized figures comprises what is known as the Great Gallery in Barrier Canyon (pls. 34–37 and figs. 73 and 74). The elaborations which occur in this unusual site and the varied painting techniques used deserve discussion. With the exception of a few of the smaller representations, all of the anthropomorphs represented in the main panel lack appendages. Their mummylike aspect is further emphasized in many cases by the skull-like visages of a number of the beings. When head-dresses occur they consist of short antennae or dot crowns. The torsos of most of the anthropomorphs are richly decorated, and to achieve this decoration the Barrier Canyon artist used various techniques. The torso of the seven-foot-tall ghost-like character, known as "The Holy Ghost," in plate 35 was painted in brown by a spatter technique which contributes to his ethereal appearance. The paint on the torsos of anthropomorphs in figures 73 and 74 was thinly applied by the artist by his fingers, a technique which created a thin background on top of which lines and dots were applied in heavier paint. In addition, in some cases lines have been incised through the more heavily painted areas and the feeling of a rich textile design has resulted. Other anthropomorphs are painted in the usual manner in heavy red pigment on top of which white dot decoration is applied. As mentioned earlier, one figure has animals painted in the chest region. Another (not illustrated) has small mummylike figures incorporated into one of the torso panels.

There are a number of smaller elements meriting consideration. Tiny quadrupeds approach one anthropomorphic figure, and another has small animals perched on his shoulders. An unusual group is a triangle of exquisitely painted mountain sheep, and to the right of this are two men with spears apparently engaged in conflict (pl. 37). The expertly drawn sheep and men in active stances contrast greatly with the immobile, mummylike forms, although they were clearly executed by the same hand. The expressive quality of line and the accuracy of the drawing present in both the sheep and the men with spears denote a high degree of observation and skill on the part of this Barrier Canyon artist. Some distance to the right is another relatively small human figure which is bent at the waist and holding something in his hands as he leans toward a mummylike being (pl. 34).

In addition to the animals listed in table 4, there is a group of about nine round-bodied mountain sheep which are pecked underneath one anthropomorphic figure. Both the painted anthropomorph and the sheep appear to have been nearly obscured by subsequent rubbing of the rock surface in this area.

SR–12–4a. To the left of the main Gallery is a small separate panel of several anthropomorphs only 14 inches tall painted with long rectangular bodies (fig. 75). Colored prints of the major portion of the panel sent to the Peabody Museum by Dean R. Brimhall of Salt Lake City and Fruita, Utah, provided an excellent opportunity to study this group in detail. Of special interest is the presence of exquisite tiny animal and bird figures around the three largest anthropomorphs. The first figure of the sequence has a tiny bird and animal at the shoulders. The next figure has a small animal painted just below shoulder level, while the third has birds flying toward the shoulders as well as an animal perched in its crown. These tiny zoomorphs do not exceed an inch in length. Below these figures is a long row composed of short lines painted with mud and a number of scratched designs mentioned on page 62 of this paper.

FIGURE 74 Life-size Great Gallery ghost figures (SR–12–4), Barrier Canyon.

PLATE 34   The Great Gallery, Barrier Canyon, SR–12–4.

PLATE 35   "The Holy Ghost" and attendants, the Great Gallery, Barrier Canyon. The torso of large ghost figure is painted with a spatter technique. He is seven feet tall. Other figures are painted in dark red. White dot decoration is visible on those on the left.

Of special significance is the presence of two figures shown in side view, which appear to be hunchbacked. They could as well be carrying large conical burden baskets. These personages hold different objects in their hands. The first has a sicklelike tool and the second holds a v-shaped device like two sticks bound at the base and splayed at the tips. Tools similar to these have been found in archaeological contexts, and these representations will be considered again in a further discussion of these paintings, page 129. To the right of the hunchbacked figures is another anthropomorph with a disproportionately large outstretched hand in which he holds a bundle of wild plants. A bird flies toward him and quadrupeds which appear to be rabbits run along his arm.

As in the Barrier Canyon panel described above, numerous tiny animal and bird figures occur in association with several large anthropomorphs. Birds delicately painted and scarcely more than an inch in length occur around the sides, shoulders, and heads of the large human figures. They also appear perched on the headgear.

Somewhat separate from the main group is a composition of small figures in which an anthropomorph only a few inches high is flanked by large and small birds. Again, wild plants are portrayed (fig. 77).

The North Wash (Crescent Creek) Painting, 42Ga443. This painting, variously known as "Cleopatra" or the "Moki Queen," is located in a deep rock shelter on North Wash about ten miles from the Colorado at the mouth of Hog Spring Can-

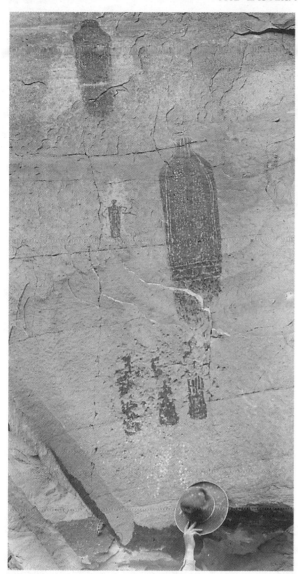

PLATE 36   Detail, the Great Gallery, Barrier Canyon.

Horse Canyon — The Bird Site. Another site in which finely drawn small figures occur is the Bird Site in Horse Canyon in the Maze area of the confluence of the Green and Colorado Rivers (fig. 76). This site is also documented in detail by Brimhall photographs. Many of the life-size anthropomorphs are highly abstract and are characterized by numerous wavy lines at their sides (see frontispiece), as are Barrier Canyon Style figures elsewhere. Certain of these figures, very reminiscent of insects, are shown with long antennalike devices as headgear and hold what appear to be wild grasses.

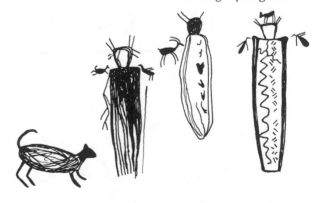

FIGURE 75   Small paintings in the Great Gallery Shelter (SR–12–4a). The anthropomorphs in this panel are only fourteen inches tall and the small birds at the shoulders of these figures do not exceed an inch in length. They are nevertheless painted with extreme care. Source: Dean Brimhall photo.

PLATE 37   Detail of mountain sheep and men with spears, the Great Gallery, Barrier Canyon. Note the elaborate torso decoration on the large anthropomorph on the right.

PLATE 38   "Cleopatra," North Wash (42Ga443). The large anthropomorph in this painting is accompanied by an acephalous animal, probably a dog. Brimhall photo.

yon. The archaeological remains found in this site are discussed below. The painting consists of a single anthropomorphic figure, five feet in height, with a companion quadruped which is acephalous (pl. 38). The human figure wears a crown of large white dots and a fillet defined by smaller ones. Hanging ornaments and earrings are also visible. The torso is further decorated with white dots and vertical stripes. The base of the figure is about ten feet above the floor of the cave.

Cottonwood Canyon, Cave Canyon, and Willow Tanks. Barrier Canyon Style paintings from Cottonwood Canyon, Cave Canyon, and Willow Tanks consist largely of dark, simple forms, most of which are badly weathered and difficult to see. Nine figures are perceivable at the Cottonwood Canyon site, but what detail there may once have been has vanished. It is apparent, however, from the sketchy remains of the designs at Cave Canyon that there was originally much more detail present here. Wild plants are again represented, and these seem to be held in the hand of an anthropomorphic figure. A long rakelike object is

also visible to the right. The Willow Tanks paintings at site SR–16–5 are in a much better state of preservation. An attenuated human figure here is painted in profile confronting a huge animal of comparable height, standing on its hind legs (fig. 78). Behind the animal are paired wavy lines and a smaller creature also in a vertical pose.

SITES OF QUESTIONABLE STYLISTIC AFFILIATION

In addition to the Barrier Canyon Style paintings discussed above, there are a few problematical sites peripheral to the main distribution of these panels, which contain anthropomorphs exhibiting characteristics of both Barrier Canyon Style and Fremont figures. In Sheep Canyon, a tributary of Nine Mile Canyon in the northern San Rafael zone, is a painted panel of four large figures which are very much like the Barrier Canyon Style paintings farther south (pl. 39). These anthropomorphs display the extreme elongation of the torso, tiny arms, and the usual horizontal band decoration characteristic of the Barrier Canyon Style figures.

PLATE 39 Painted anthropomorphs, Sheep Canyon, tributary to Nine Mile. Figures in this panel bear resemblances to both Barrier Canyon Style and Fremont work.

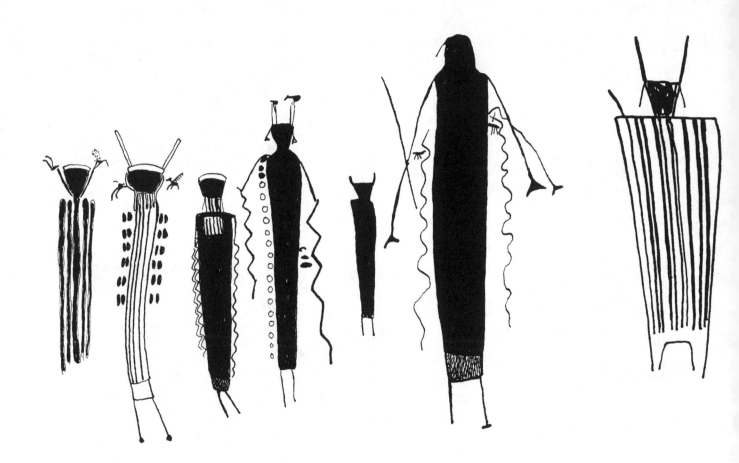

FIGURE 76 The Bird Site Paintings, Horse Canyon. The anthropomorphs at this site are greater than life-size. Again, there are small animals and birds at the sides of the figures. Source: Dean Brimhall photo.

The simple head decoration consisting of a white crown and antennae on the two central figures is also typical. Features reminiscent of Fremont anthropomorphs are the short curved horns and the yoke element on the right end anthropomorph.

On Trachyte Creek are three triangular anthropomorphs painted in yellow. These are not elongated in shape, but one figure wears a crown resembling the Barrier Canyon mode of head decoration.

Lacking any distinctive features are the faded red paintings of large anthropomorphic figures with tiny heads and long rectangular bodies from Black Dragon Canyon, Buckhorn, and Range Creek (fig. 79). The only elaborations present are the simple horns of feathered headdresses on the Range Creek pair and the possible hair whorls on the Buckhorn example. The Range Creek figures are accompanied by a large quadruped. These paintings are very similar to the unornamented, red anthropomorphic figures from Thompson described by Morss (1931, p. 39) on which Fremont material was clearly superimposed (see page 42, this paper).

The significance of these ambiguous simple heroic anthropomorphs and those displaying both Barrier Canyon Style and Fremont traits is not clear at the present time. It does, however, appear that in a few rare instances transitional figures between the Barrier Canyon Style and Fremont anthropomorphs do exist. The possibilities latent in this phenomenon will be considered below.

FIGURE 77 Small painting at the Bird Site, Horse Canyon. The large anthropomorph in this panel is not more than eight inches tall. As in the large painting at this site, wild plants and small zoomorphs are present. Source: Dean Brimhall photo and E. J. Bird drawing.

FIGURE 78 Barrier Canyon Style paintings, Willow Tanks.

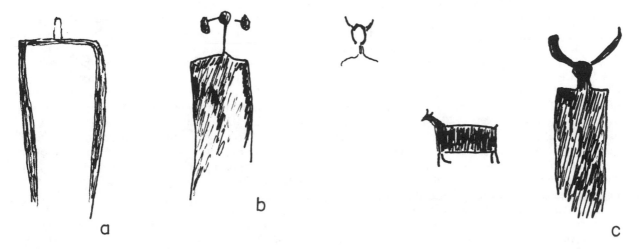

FIGURE 79 Faded red anthropomorphs lacking distinctive features from a, Black Dragon Canyon, Site 33; b, Buckhorn, and c, Range Creek. The Buckhorn figure (b) is greater than life size. Beckwith photo.

IV

Rock Art West of the Wasatch Mountains

Having discussed the Fremont rock art of the Colorado Plateau and other stylistic manifestations in the Fremont area of eastern Utah, I will continue with a description of Fremont rock art and associated styles as they occur on the eastern edge of the Basin and Range province in the western part of the state and eastern Nevada (fig. 80). With the exception of the high ranges of central Utah which border this area on the east, the boundaries of the western Fremont division do not follow rivers and other rugged geographic features as they did for the eastern Fremont area. As mentioned earlier, this area is characterized by semiarid interior drainage basins and encompasses three major deserts: the Great Salt Lake Desert in northwestern Utah and the Sevier-Black Rock Desert and the Escalante Desert in the central and southern portions.

Archaeologically, western Utah is well known for its Fremont remains. Hunting and gathering bands, however, preceded the Fremont culture in western Utah and followed after its decline. Evidence of thousands of years of occupation by early hunting and gathering peoples is abundant in sites falling within the Desert Culture category (Steward 1937a, Rudy 1953, Jennings and Norbeck 1955, Jennings 1957, and Aikens 1970). A well-documented summary of the early occupation of the Great Salt Lake region can be found in Wormington (1955, pp. 110–113). These earlier groups may be responsible for the large numbers of Great Basin Curvilinear Style petroglyph sites prevalent throughout western Utah.

Rock art sites recorded from the Great Salt Lake region are relatively few, and the paucity of panels even possibly attributable to Fremont origin here is consistent with the general archaeological picture. In a survey of this area by Rudy, none of the Fremont sites examined indicated the presence of large groups of people or a long occupation (Wormington 1955, p. 117). The file data on this region are largely a compilation of previously published work. Farther south in central-western Utah, Fremont rock art material is substantial only from the Clear Creek drainage, although other scattered sites are noted (fig. 80).

Within western Utah, three major styles are recognized. The Western Utah Painted Style has been recorded primarily from the vicinity of Great Salt Lake but also occurs from as far south as Fool Creek (fig. 80). Petroglyphs in the central-western Utah region consisting of solidly carved, often decorative, elements which reflect in many instances a Virgin Kayenta derivation are classed as Sevier Style A. A third group of petroglyphs of considerable significance represents the Great Basin Curvilinear Style (Heizer and Baumhoff 1962). This last style, as such, is not attributable to the Fremont culture. The relevance of this style to the Fremont problem, however, is brought out by the observation that there seems to have been a mingling of the Curvilinear Style and Fremont motifs in western Utah. The nature of this association and the problems involved will be considered below. Finally, Fremont sites in eastern Nevada are distinctive in their simplicity and in their treatment of the Fremont anthropomorph.

Before discussing the styles delineated above in more detail, a word should be added about the Great Basin Representational Style defined by Heizer and Baumhoff for Nevada sites (1962, pp. 202–205). This style as such is not recognized here since it does not conform to the concept of a culturally determined style as used. Heizer and Baumhoff include in this grouping all representational elements occurring in the Great Basin, encompassing not only the stylistically divergent Fremont and Virgin Kayenta Anasazi petroglyphs in this area, but also isolated examples of representational figures in western Nevada which are typologically at variance with both the Pueblo and Fremont material.

THE WESTERN UTAH PAINTED STYLE

The Western Utah Painted Style is at this time a tentative category, the validity of which remains to be established. As defined here, it is distinguished by the simple painted representation, usually in red, of a Fremont-like triangular-bodied horned anthropomorph. The style as currently conceived is best represented in the Salt Lake region, where a small number of sites have been recorded (fig. 80). In Cave 1 on Promontory Point, there are three figures painted in red (fig. 81). Two represent horned anthropomorphs with triangular bodies, short legs, and jointed arms. The largest figure is fifteen inches tall. The third design is a crude rendition of a zoomorphic form which, although it has but two legs, appears to be a mountain sheep. Upon excavation the cave yielded no Fremont remains, but the most recent occupation was that of the Promontory Culture. Aikens (1966b, pp. 74–75) has used this situation to support his thesis of a close relationship or identity between the Northern Utah Fremont and the Promontory Culture. No other caves in the vicinity contained Fremont material or further paintings.

Additional red paintings of triangular and trapezoidal men have been described by Sleight (1946, pp. 88–92) from fourteen miles west of Corinne, Utah, and by Judd (1926, p. 10) from the vicinity of Willard. Finally, anthropomorphs in this style are documented from Fool Creek in west-central Utah (fig. 82).

Whether or not to include in this style painted panels of anthropomorphic handprints, and geometric pottery and textilelike designs such as those from Fool Creek (fig. 83) and the Clear Creek drainage (fig. 84 and pl. 40) is highly debatable. These panels bear an overall resemblance to others in Sevier Style A and are perhaps more rightly classified in that category.

There are also other types of paintings from the Great Salt Lake region recorded by Sleight (1946) and Steward (1937a, p. 87) consisting of circle clusters, plain and bisected circles, dot rows, ladders, zigzags, parallel-line motifs, and diamond-shaped designs, all of which are prominent elements in the Great Basin Curvilinear Style and are also found in Fremont panels throughout Utah.

PLATE 40 Red painted design, Clear Creek Canyon. Beckwith photo, Panel B 35.

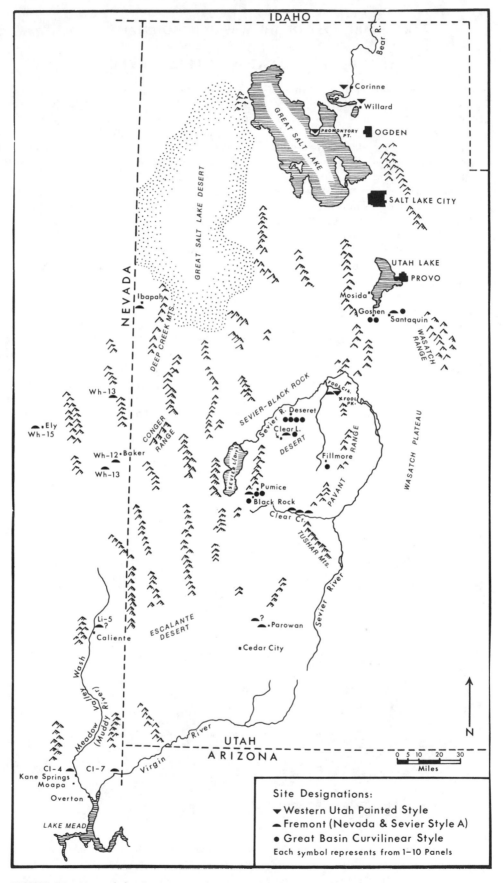

FIGURE 80 Map of the Fremont area west of the Wasatch Mountains showing rock art site locations. Locations are approximate.

SEVIER STYLE A

Sevier Style A is the western Fremont style most closely resembling Fremont styles in the eastern area. Within the documented materials, Clear Creek, a tributary of the Sevier River flowing eastward through a gap between the Tushar Mountains and the Pavant Range, is the type district in which this style occurs.

The elements from the Clear Creek sites are tabulated in table 5. At the site popularly referred to as "Newspaper Rock" (pl. 41), it is difficult to tell whether Curvilinear Style elements appearing here are an integral part of Sevier Style A, having been adopted by Fremont artists, or whether they have a separate origin. Judging from the large number of superimpositions in this panel, the site must have been used over a long period of time. Also, the painted geometric motifs mentioned above are included in the tabulation since they are stylistically consistent with the appearance of other decorative abstract elements in Sevier Style A. On the whole, the summary data are generally representative of the elements of this style.

The Fremont petroglyphs of Sevier Style A are characterized by compact arrangements of small, solidly carved elements (figs. 85–87 and pls. 41–43). These figures are often neatly pecked and the panels display an interest in the qualities of design effected by the use of clear-cut shapes and in contrasts between solidly carved and open areas. Anthropomorphic figures make up 11 percent of the total element inventory of the Sevier A Style sites (table 5 and fig. 7). This is the lowest rate of occurrence of this element in any of the Fremont styles.

The anthropomorphic figure appears as a dominant element (pl. 43) in only two of the photographs (in the files), although a series of Beckwith drawings of Clear Creek anthropomorphs (fig. 88) suggests that it may occur as a dominant element in other sites as well. (These latter figures, incidentally, are not included in the tabulations, because they appear out of context.) Large as well as small figures are often solidly carved and the triangular body form occurs over three times as often as the trapezoidal. Even the trapezoidal figures are often strongly tapered toward the triangular. A new feature appearing on the western anthropomorphs is the addition to the torso of a basal element which may take the form of another but smaller triangle, or a square or boat-shaped object (figs. 87 and 88). A variation on this theme may be created by drawing a line at right angles to the base of the torso and from the

ends of this line suspending the legs, again at right angles (fig. 85). Elaborations are few. Except for an occasional vertical central line through the body, torso decoration is absent. Hands and feet when represented are simply suggested by a few sketchy lines. Certain figures, however, are shown carrying simple objects. Roughly one-quarter of the anthropomorphs are horned, and plumes, facial features, and earbobs are rare phenomena.

Quadrupeds constitute a higher percentage of the elements present in Sevier Style A, making up 28 percent of the total. Nearly all of these are solidly carved, and more than half are recognizable as mountain sheep. Birds, tracks, and hand- or footprints make up the remainder of the representative designs.

Abstract elements occur in larger numbers in this style than in any other rock art style attributable to Fremont origin, making up 52 percent, or over half, of the element inventory. Forty-two percent of these were random figures which could not be categorized. Among those identifiable, wavy lines, spirals, and dots or dot designs again rank as most popular. It should be noted that the wavy line in these sites may occur as a double-lined rather than a single-lined motif. Also appearing for the first time are the compact pottery or textilelike designs, the rectilinear spiral, and nested chevrons, all of which occur in small percentages (table 5).

The Sevier Style A is also identifiable from a few sites outside of the Clear Creek drainage. The Fool Creek paintings (fig. 83) of abstract pottery- and textilelike motifs were mentioned above (p. 85). At Clear Lake, an extensive petroglyph site carved on an old lava flow displays panels of both Sevier Style A and Great Basin Curvilinear Style figures. The Sevier type figures present here consist of widely spaced representations of mountain sheep and other quadrupeds and small anthropomorphs (fig. 89). The anthropomorphic shape is generally triangular and in one instance there is a boat-shaped appendage at the base. The animals are crudely carved and vary between being fullbodied representations and stick figures. Among the elements at the opposite end of the site (fig. 90) appears a triangular anthropomorph in outline which seems to be a part of the Curvilinear Style complex with which it appears, and not of Sevier Style A. In Summit Canyon near Santaquin (42Ut148), key motifs resembling pottery decoration and figures composing a scene of a mountain sheep hunt are stylistically more akin to Sevier Style A than to the Curvilinear elements carved nearby (figs. 91 and 92). Finally, Sevier Style A type figures consisting of two mountain sheep and a double wavy line appear in one panel at Black Rock in conjunction with Curvilinear Style elements, with which they appear to be contemporary (pl. 44).

Although the affinity of these representational figures with Sevier Style A seems obvious, there is a certain classification problem in some of the Great Basin sites of western Utah, because of the fact that there is a typological continuum between the solid Sevier Style A figures which appear here from time to time and the stick figure representational elements which have become an integral part of the Curvilinear Style. The problems involved are discussed in the following section.

FIGURE 81 Figures in the Western Utah Painted Style, Cave 1, Promontory Point. Source: Steward 1937a, pp. 87–88.

FIGURE 82 Anthropomorphs in the Western Utah Painted Style, Fool Creek. Source: Beckwith drawing.

FIGURE 83 Painted geometric designs, Fool Creek. Source: Beckwith photo, Panel B 62.

FIGURE 84 Painted anthropomorph, handprints, and decorative designs, Clear Creek Canyon. Source: Beckwith photo, Panel B 50.

PLATE 41   Petroglyphs, "Newspaper Rock," Sevier Style A, Clear Creek Canyon. Beckwith notes that there are between 200 to 300 carvings on this rock. Beckwith photo, Panel B 49.

FIGURE 85   Sevier Style A petroglyphs, Clear Creek Canyon. Source: Beckwith-Steward photo, Panel BS 2.

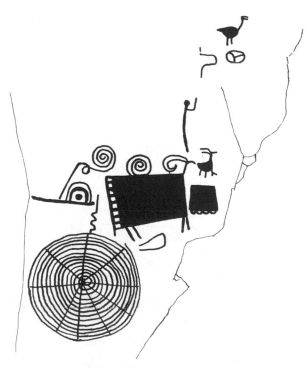

FIGURE 86   Sevier Style A petroglyphs, Clear Creek Canyon. Source: Beckwith photo, Panel B 57.

THE FREMONT AND THE GREAT BASIN CURVILINEAR STYLE

As mentioned above, the sites in western Utah in which small horned anthropomorphic figures and other representational elements appear in conjunction with Great Basin Curvilinear Style petroglyphs deserve consideration here. The Great Basin Curvilinear Style originally defined by Steward (1929, p. 220) and later discussed in some detail by Heizer and Baumhoff (1962) is said to be characterized by the presence of the circle, concentric circles, chains of circles, sun disks, curvilinear meanders, stars, and snakes (Heizer and Baumhoff 1962, p. 200). In elaborating, they say: "The circle, in one context or another, is the common element of this style but perhaps a more characteristic element is the curvilinear meander. These meanders have a vague sort of composition in that they tend to fill an area defined by the outline of a single boulder. But aside from two restrictions — curving lines without abrupt discontinuities and spatial restrictions provided by the areas of a single boulder face — there seems to be no aesthetic discipline imposed on the style" (1962, p. 205). The elements in the Curvilinear Style sites of western Utah are tabulated in table 6 and further summarized in figure 7. The style consisting of abstract elements as described and illustrated by these authors is prevalent in west-

ern Utah in exemplary form, as seen in certain panels from Deseret and Black Rock (figs. 93–95 and pls. 45–48). Nevertheless, as many as 66 percent of the western Utah Curvilinear Style sites are characterized by the presence of a few representational figures. It is notable, however, that in spite of their wide distribution they constitute only 17 percent of the total element inventory (table 6). These representational designs can be grouped into two general categories, although as noted above, a continuous range of figure types is present: 1) those which maintain at least in part a typological resemblance to the Fremont elements and 2) those which have been reduced to stick-figure linear elements, stylistically an integral part of the Great Basin Curvilinear Style configuration. Representational elements in figures 96 and 97 are representative of the first situation while figures 98–101 and plate 49 illustrate examples of the second. A combination of events can be seen in figures 102–104.

Representational subject matter in either instance consists largely of mountain sheep and anthropomorphs, and an occasional hand- or footprint may also be depicted. The lack of trapezoidal anthropomorphs and the rarity of triangular ones are notable here, although more

FIGURE 87 Sevier Style A petroglyphs, Clear Creek Canyon. Source: Beckwith-Steward photo, Panel BS 1.

FIGURE 88 Representative examples of anthropomorphic figures from Clear Creek Canyon. Source: Beckwith drawing.

FIGURE 89 Sevier Style A petroglyphs, Clear Lake. Source: Beckwith photo, Panel B 65.

FIGURE 90 Great Basin Curvilinear panel with stylized anthropomorph, Clear Lake. Source: Beckwith photo, Panel B 65.

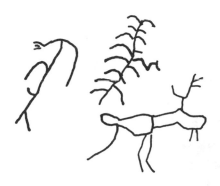

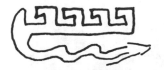

FIGURE 91 Petroglyphs, Summit Canyon, Santaquin (42Ut148). Source: Putnam 1876, pl. 28.

than half of these figures bear horns (table 6). Quadrupeds listed as solid in table 6 may be thinner bodied than solid representations from other styles. A large proportion of both anthropomorphic figures and quadrupeds are stick-figure representations, which are often highly schematic. At times the degree of abstraction is so great that, were it not for the presence of horns on these figures, their status as a representational element would go unrecognized.

On the basis of the current data, it seems reasonable to suggest that those representative elements, scattered among Great Basin Curvilinear Style elements but showing at least partial typological resemblance to Fremont types, may eventually be found to constitute a second Sevier

Fremont stylistic manifestation which might be termed Sevier Style B. At the current time, there is little way to judge whether or not these figures were made contemporaneously with the accompanying Curvilinear Style designs or whether they are later additions by Fremont people. As for the second situation, in which the representational figures are actually incorporated into the Curvilinear Style framework and in which little vestige of Fremont figure types remain, it is suggested that these panels be regarded as a variety of the Great Basin Curvilinear Style. In this case it appears that the Curvilinear rock artists were influenced by the Fremont culture, and the incorporation of representational designs into an otherwise abstract art may take on temporal significance for the archaeologist.

PLATE 42 Petroglyphs, Sevier Style A, Clear Creek Canyon, Beckwith-Steward photo, Panel B 60.

FIGURE 92 Petroglyphs, Summit Canyon, Santaquin (42Ut148). Source: Putnam 1876, pl. 28.

PLATE 43 Petroglyphs, Sevier Style A, Clear Creek Canyon. Beckwith-Steward photo, Panel B 56.

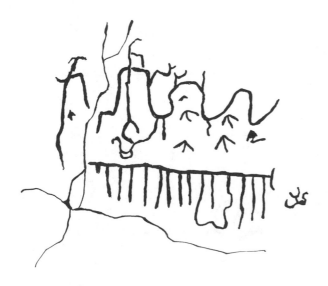

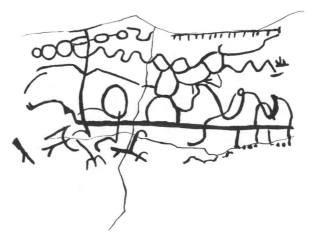

FIGURE 93 Petroglyphs, Great Basin Curvilinear Style, Deseret. Source: Beckwith-Steward photo, Panel BS 3.

FIGURE 94 Petroglyphs, Great Basin Curvilinear Style, Black Rock. Source: Beckwith photo, Panel B 105.

PLATE 44 Petroglyphs, Sevier Style A and Curvilinear Style designs, Black Rock. Panel was partially chalked before photographing. Beckwith photo, Panel B 129.

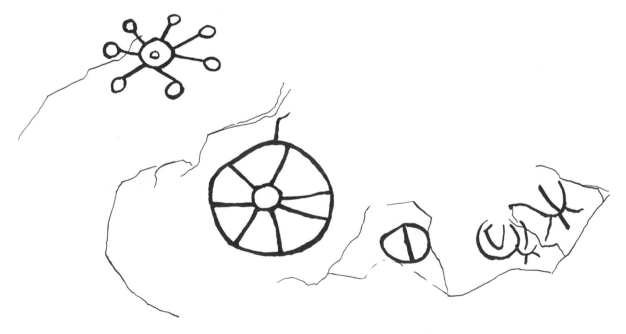

FIGURE 95 Petroglyphs, Great Basin Curvilinear Style, Deseret. Source: Beckwith photo B 148.

FIGURE 96 Petroglyphs, Great Basin Curvilinear Style and representational figures, Pumice. Source: Beckwith photo, Panel B 110.

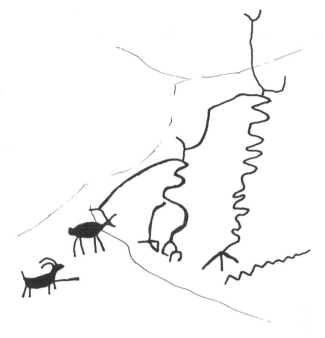

FIGURE 97 Petroglyphs, Great Basin Curvilinear Style and mountain sheep. Black Rock. Source: Beckwith photo, Panel B 118.

PLATE 45 Petroglyphs, Great Basin Curvilinear Style, Black Rock. Beckwith photo, Panel B 105.

FIGURE 98 A selection of anthropomorphic figures from Mosida, modified from Fremont types in a Curvilinear Style direction. Source: Beckwith drawing.

PLATE 46 Petroglyphs, Great Basin Curvilinear Style, Black Rock. Beckwith photo, Panel B 124.

PLATE 47 Petroglyphs, Great Basin Curvilinear Style, Deseret. Beckwith photo, Panel N 156.

FIGURE 99 Petroglyphs, Great Basin Curvilinear Style with representational elements, Fillmore. Source: Beckwith photo, Panel B 130.

PETROGLYPHS AT PAROWAN GAP AND BRAFFET CANYON

Before leaving the discussion of the rock art of the Fremont area of Western Utah, I need to say a word about two additional sites in the vicinity of Parowan on the eastern edge of the Escalante Desert (fig. 80). The first and most important site, located in "The Gap," seven miles west of Parowan, has a number of unusual characteristics (fig. 105 and pls. 50 and 51). With so few sites on record from this vicinity, it is impossible to know at this juncture whether the unusual features of these panels are a local manifestation or whether this site is somewhat typical of the Parowan district. The petroglyphs have previously been discussed and illustrated by Judd (1926, p. 38, pl. 4), Steward (1937b, pl. 10), and Greenwood (1956, pp. 109–118); but little which is conclusive has been said. Judd states that the greater part of the designs are of Shoshonean origin, but there is very little to back up this contention. There is apparently a great deal of superimposition and

PLATE 48 Petroglyphs, Great Basin Curvilinear Style, Deseret. Beckwith-Steward photo, Panel B 165.

FIGURE 100 Petroglyphs, Great Basin Curvilinear Style with quadruped, Deseret. Source: Beckwith-Steward photo, Panel BS 6.

FIGURE 101 Petroglyphs, Deseret. Source: Beckwith photo, Panel B 149.

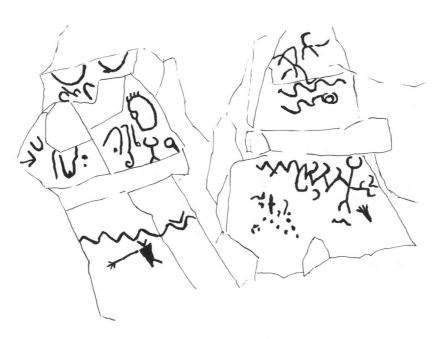

FIGURE 102 Petroglyphs, Great Basin Curvilinear Style with anthropomorphs, Mosida. Source: Beckwith photo, Panel B 167.

PLATE 49 Petroglyphs, Great Basin Curvilinear Style with representational elements, Deseret. Beckwith photo, Panel B 155.

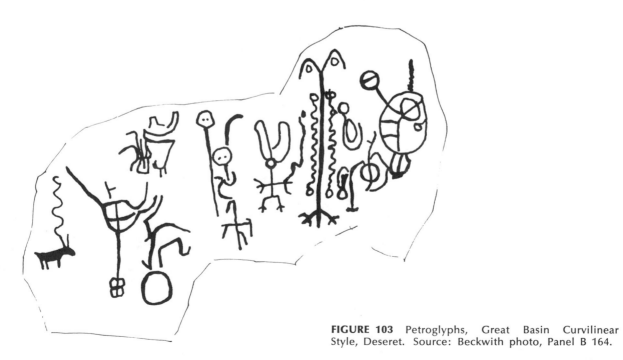

FIGURE 103 Petroglyphs, Great Basin Curvilinear Style, Deseret. Source: Beckwith photo, Panel B 164.

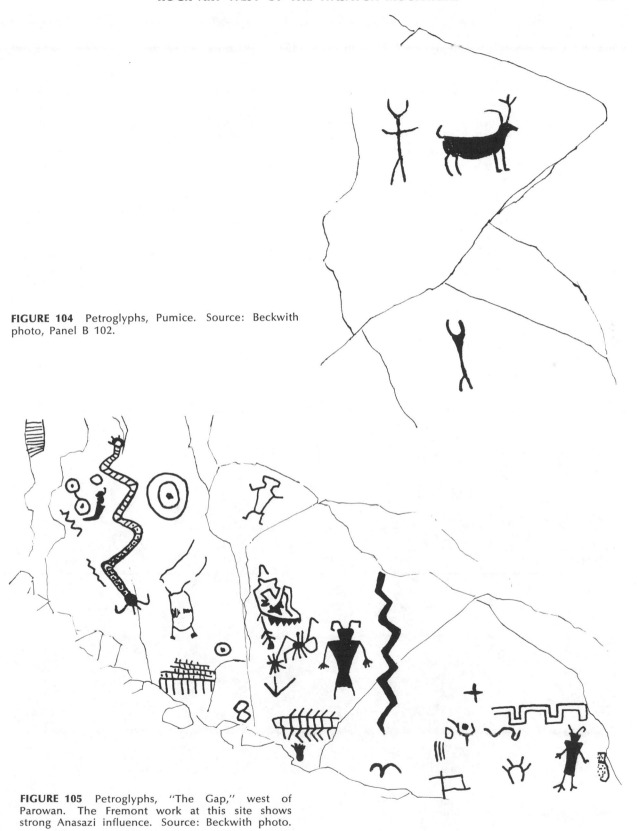

FIGURE 104 Petroglyphs, Pumice. Source: Beckwith photo, Panel B 102.

FIGURE 105 Petroglyphs, "The Gap," west of Parowan. The Fremont work at this site shows strong Anasazi influence. Source: Beckwith photo.

variation in degree of weathering between figures, indicating that the site was used for petroglyph-making over a long period of time. To unwind these superimpositions from photographs, however, is almost impossible.

The carvings here exhibit an uncommon degree of tidiness and are unusual in their textural effects created by the close juxtaposition of small repeated elements such as finely carved lines and rows of dots (pl. 50). Such elements are often enclosed in a small area in which they create the effect of a sculptured surface. It is not surprising in a locality where so much interest is expressed in surface effect to find a zigzag (possibly a serpent) carved in bas-relief (pl. 51).

A certain number of elements appear here which heretofore have not been encountered.

Among these are the extended two-pole ladders, large square or rectangular blocks enclosing rows of dots or other simple designs, dotted grids, and solid circles surrounded by a dot ring (fig. 105 and pl. 50). Joined circles, rakes, concentric circles, sun discs, spirals, wavy lines, and zigzags, and sawtooth motifs, well known from both Fremont and Curvilinear Style sites, are also carved here, but with an unusual degree of precision and clarity. In addition, there are distinctly Fremont elements such as the trapezoidal-bodied horned anthropomorphs.

A second site, in Braffet Canyon two or three miles west of Parowan, displays elements represented in Fremont sites elsewhere in western Utah. A rectilinear spiral, a circle with sawtooth decoration, and a scorpion motif are present (fig. 106).

PLATE 50 Petroglyphs, at "The Gap," west of Parowan. Panel exhibits an unusual variety of figures and many superimpositions, Beckwith photo.

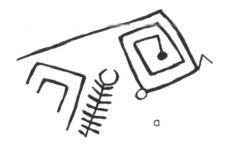 

FIGURE 106   Petroglyphs, Braffet Canyon, west of Parowan. Source: Beckwith photo.

PLATE 51   Serpentine design carved in bas-relief, "The Gap," west of Parowan. Beckwith photo.

FREMONT SITES IN EASTERN NEVADA

Eastern Nevada sites displaying Fremont type figures were set aside for separate discussion, as they seem to manifest a number of their own peculiarities which distinguish them from those of other regions. With the exception of the single site near Ibapah, Utah, all of the sites currently under consideration are scattered along the eastern border of Nevada between Ely and Overton (fig. 80). Most of these have been described or illustrated in previous publications. The Sans Creek figures near Ibapah have been discussed by Reagan (1917, pp. 30 and 32). The Baker Creek Cave sites have been reported by Steward (1929, pp. 145–146), E. P. Harrington (1933), M. R. Harrington (1934), Vogel (1952), and Heizer and Baumhoff (1962, pp. 69–70, fig. 130, and fig. 131 a and b). Kachina Rock Shelter, 35 miles north of Baker, is described by M. R. Harrington (1932) and Heizer and Baumhoff (1962, fig. 131 c–f). Mosier Canyon paintings near Ely are also illustrated by Heizer and Baumhoff (fig. 131 d). From Clark County in southeastern Nevada, Fremont figures documented in the Scott files have been illustrated by Steward (1929, fig. 90 c and d) and by Heizer and Baumhoff (1962, figs. 62 b–e and 65 a and b). Heizer and Baumhoff's figures 65 a and 130 a illustrate panels of simple figures said to be from the Virgin River district in Clark County and Upper Baker Creek Cave from White Pine County, respectively. As these panels are essentially identical it is felt that a single panel may be involved and that there may be an error in regard to location in one of the original sources (Steward 1929, pl. 93 c, and E. P. Harrington 1933). Finally, recent investigations in Lincoln County have revealed what may be Fremont type figures in the Stein Shelter (Fowler 1970).

On the whole, the eastern Nevada Fremont work appears to consist largely of painted representations of the Fremont anthropomorph (figs. 107–114 and pl. 52). The simplest anthropomorphic types (figs. 107–111) are portrayed with triangular or trapezoidal torsos, although the former shape is usually preferred. Rudimentary arms and legs may be indicated with short lines, and the figures frequently have horns or other simple headgear. The basal triangular element or line drawn perpendicular to the body axis may

PLATE 52 Painted anthropomorphs, Kane Springs, Clark County, Nevada, Cl–4. Photo source unknown.

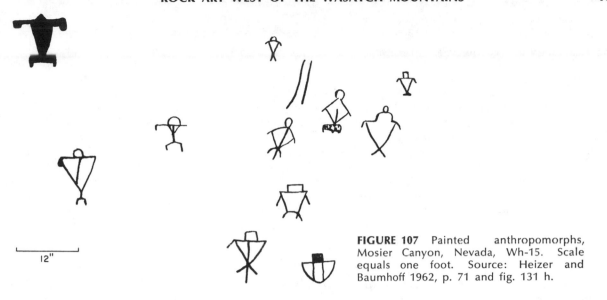

FIGURE 107 Painted anthropomorphs, Mosier Canyon, Nevada, Wh-15. Scale equals one foot. Source: Heizer and Baumhoff 1962, p. 71 and fig. 131 h.

FIGURE 108 Painted figures, Baker Creek, Nevada, Wh-12. Scale equals one foot. Source: Heizer and Baumhoff 1962, figs. 130 l and 131 a and b.

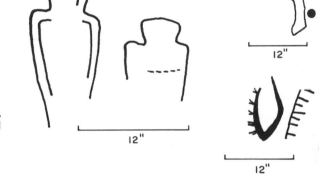

FIGURE 109 Painted anthropomorphs, Upper Baker Creek Cave, Nevada, Wh-3. Source: Heizer and Baumhoff, fig. 130 a.

be represented. Further torso decoration may be a vertical center line or interior lines closely paralleling the outlines of the head and body.

More complex figures appearing in both the southern and central eastern Nevada sites tend to have long tapering triangular bodies (figs. 112–114). These figures have ample rectangular heads which may be separated from the torso by a single line for the neck. The head may be embellished with fringed horns, and a distinctive line or dot facial decoration arranged without regard for features is a peculiarity appearing on these figures. Further fringing may occur on the arms and torsos, and in two instances anthropomorphs hold small shields and other objects. Paintings from the widely separated sites of Kachina Rock Shelter near Baker and Kane Springs in Clark County are nearly identical in these elaborations (fig. 112 and pl. 52). Other anthropomorphs from Kane Springs are depicted with hairbobs or earrings (fig. 114).

In most of the panels on record, the anthropomorph appears with few associated elements. Assuming, however, that the mountain sheep, snakes, and the variety of dots, lines, and zigzags appearing in the Stein Shelter (Fowler 1970) are contemporary with the Fremont type anthropomorphs, this site may be a major exception to this observation. Fowler (1970) also mentions that some of the larger figures reaching an estimated five to six feet in height are buried up to their shoulders in alluvium.

The apparent distinctiveness of the rock art of the western edge of the Fremont area lends certain support to the separate designation of this region by Ambler (1966a), who labeled it the "Conger Fremont." On the basis of recent excavations in the southern part of the region, however, the validity of this as a separable cultural region within the Fremont area has recently been called into question by Fowler (1970) and by Ambler himself (1970).

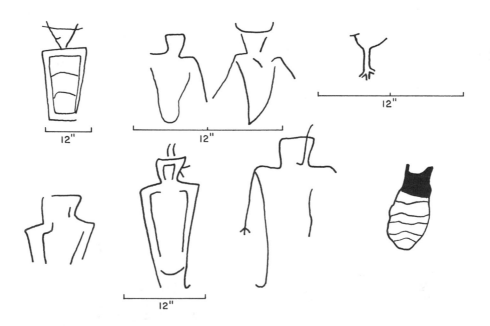

FIGURE 110   Painted anthropomorphs, Upper Baker Creek Cave, Nevada, Wh-3. Scales equal one foot. Source: Heizer and Baumhoff, fig. 130 b–h.

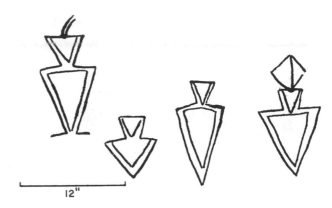

FIGURE 111 Painted anthropomorphs, Virgin River, Nevada, Cl-7 (or Upper Baker Creek Cave — see text). Scale equals one foot. Source: Steward 1929, pl. 93 d.

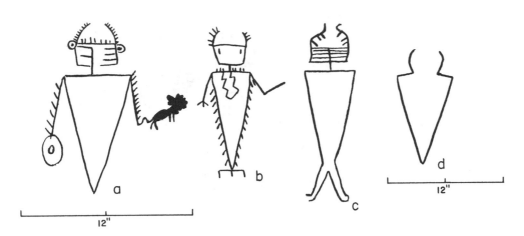

FIGURE 112 Complex painted anthropomorphic designs from Kachina Rock Shelter, north of Baker, Nevada, Wh-13. Scales equal one foot. Source: Heizer and Baumhoff, fig. 131 c–f.

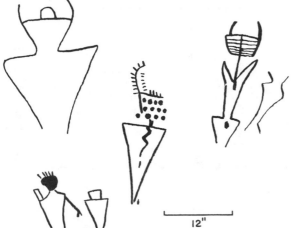

FIGURE 113 Complex painted anthropomorphic designs, Kane Springs, Clark County, Nevada, Cl-4. Scale equals one foot. Source: Anonymous photo.

12"

FIGURE 114 Anthropomorphic   paintings,   Kane
Springs, Nevada, CI-4. Scale equals one foot. Source:
Anonymous photo.

V

Summary

In the foregoing discussion, we have seen that within the general configuration of Fremont rock art a number of styles may be distinguished which in the case of the Fremont east of the Wasatch correspond broadly to the regional divisions perceived on the basis of other archaeological data. Throughout, the hallmark of Fremont authorship is seen in the presence of broad-shouldered anthropomorphs of trapezoidal or triangular shape, and these figures typically wear horned headdresses. In several regions such anthropomorphic representations may approximate life size. Present also among Fremont designs are mountain sheep, bison, deer, shields, and numerous abstract elements.

In the eastern Fremont the broad-shouldered anthropomorph is typically trapezoidal in form but manifests a large number of variations. This figure is frequently masked or has facial features indicated and is shown wearing elaborate headgear and necklaces. Kilt, sashes, and torso decoration are often depicted. Shield figures are also present throughout the entire eastern area. The climax of Fremont rock art development is apparent in the Classic Vernal Style in which the carved anthropomorphic figure is exquisitely rendered in outline form and reaches a peak of elaboration and variety. Forms are basically geometric and tend to be executed with precision. Detailed elaboration is often in the form of the dot decoration typical of this district. An interest in the design qualities of the figures is manifested throughout. Most closely affiliated with the Classic Vernal anthropomorphs are those from the Fremont River district of the southern San Rafael region, which, although less complex, have characteristics in common with the northern figures. In addition, there are a number of painted southern San Rafael anthropomorphs which exhibit an unusual number of traits found in the Fremont figurine tradition. The intervening northern San Rafael zone is characterized less by the dominant Fremont anthropomorph and more by the large numbers of small solidly carved representational elements and a proliferation of abstract designs.

West of the Wasatch Mountains, Fremont rock art is less well documented than in the eastern regions; nevertheless, certain stylistic groupings have been distinguished on the basis of the data available. The area around the Great Salt Lake as currently known is characterized primarily by the Western Utah Painted Style, while in central western Utah, petroglyph panels displaying Anasazi-derived elements are common. The latter panels are designated as Sevier Style A. In many of the Great Basin sites throughout western Utah, however, the Puebloan elements are largely dropped. Horned Fremont-like anthropomorphs and other representational figures occur in association with the Curvilinear Style and take on to varying degrees the overall linear and whimsical qualities characteristic of this style. Fremont sites in eastern Nevada are characterized by their simplicity and certain distinctive decorative features of the anthropomorphic figure.

With the exception of the two known examples in Nevada, the shield and shield-bearing figure is generally absent in the western area of Fremont activity. The western Fremont anthropomorph, although devoid of the rampant elaboration of its eastern counterpart, displays a number of characteristics peculiar to the area. The triangular body shape is preferred over the trapezoidal and the figure is often distinguished by a horizontal line, triangle, rectangle, or boat-shaped appendage attached to the base of the body triangle. Large Fremont anthropomorphs which dominate the panels in which they occur were found to be largely confined to the Clear Creek district, where they may attain a height of over five feet.

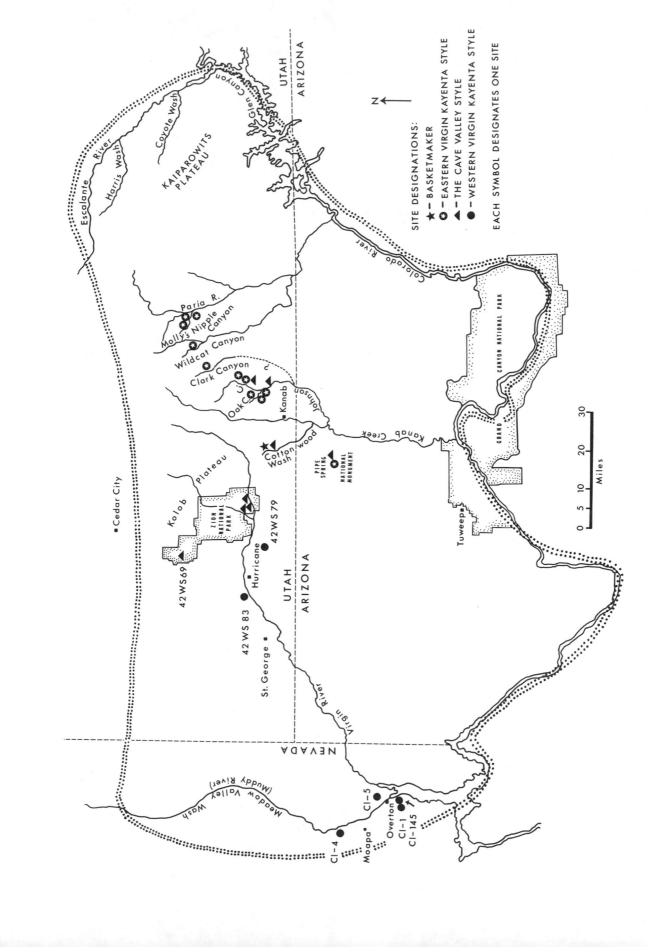

FIGURE 115 Map of the Virgin Kayenta division of the Anasazi (after Aikens 1966b, fig. 1, and Steward 1941, fig. 26) with rock art sites indicated. Site locations are approximate.

V I

Rock Art of the
Virgin Kayenta Region of the Anasazi

The second major rock art complex to be considered in this study is that of the Virgin division of the Puebloan peoples. Immediately south of the western Fremont area, the Virgin domain once extended throughout southern Utah west of the Escalante River and western Arizona north of the Colorado River, a region known as the Arizona Strip, and into the adjacent parts of southeastern Nevada (fig. 115). Geographically the area embraces the western extension of the high mesas and canyon lands of the Colorado Plateau and, west of Zion, the broad valleys and parallel fault-block ranges of the Great Basin.

The Virgin division manifests temporal developments analogous to those of other Anasazi areas. Phases equivalent to Basketmaker II through early Pueblo III have been named and described by various investigators (Colton 1952, Shutler 1961, and Aikens 1966a). It is generally recognized, however, that with the exception of the Moapa phase material in Nevada (Shutler 1961, p. 67), the Cave du Pont material from near Kanab (Nusbaum 1922), and possibly Schroeder's ZNP–21 site at Zion (Schroeder 1955, pp. 76–99), the evidence for a Basketmaker II phase of development is meager. Also, the Pueblo I phase as it occurs in the Virgin region is somewhat vague due to the persistence here of Basketmaker III traits until Pueblo II times. The Virgin people appear to have lived a Basketmaker III sort of existence until around A.D. 1000, when they rapidly received strong Pueblo II influences while still retaining many anachronistic traits (Ambler 1966a).

The nature of the relationship of the Virgin division to the larger Anasazi picture has been a question of some debate. Ceramic studies by Colton revealed that pottery types of the "Arizona Strip" north of the Colorado River grade imper-

ceptibly into those of southwestern Utah (1952, p. 3). In a more recent study based on the cultural model of Daifuku for Southwestern cultures, Aikens (1966a) as the result of phase to phase comparisons of the total cultural inventory, stresses that there is a continuity of basic cultural patterns throughout the Pueblo history of the Kayenta and Virgin Anasazi from Basic Southwestern to Florescent times. Similar systems of social organization, subsistence and technology, ceremony and recreation, and clothing and ornaments are emphasized. In the latter part of the Florescent stage, however, between A.D. 900 and 1100, a certain divergence begins to occur between the Kayenta and Virgin areas, as evidenced by differences in site layout, architectural details, and certain ceramic attributes.

The Virgin division was originally given "branch" status within the Anasazi culture by Gladwin and Gladwin (1934), who grouped the Anasazi of southern Utah and Nevada under the designation of Nevada Branch. This term was later modified by Colton (1952, p. 5) to the Virgin Branch, which embraced the prehistoric pueblo cultures found in the Arizona Strip as well as those of southwestern Utah and southern Nevada. Recently the validity of the designation of the Virgin culture as a separate branch of the Anasazi has been called into question. On the basis of ceramic analysis, Florence Lister (1964, p. 66) has suggested the abandonment of the concept of the Virgin Branch. She feels, as does Aikens, that the Virgin Anasazi is an unspecialized variant of the Kayenta Branch with pottery and other traits differing from those of the central Kayenta area only in minor details, and points out that intense Virgin regional specializations are lacking. Thus, she suggests a subbranch designation of the Virgin area. Following this view as well as Ambler's suggestion (1966a, p. 174) that the Virgin Anasazi be distinguished by a qualifying term to differentiate it from the San Juan Kayenta, the Virgin division will hereafter be referred to as the "Virgin Kayenta."

Within the Virgin Kayenta territory there are certain regional cultural variations to be considered. Schroeder (1955, table 1), for example, illustrates that the ceramic complex, architectural features, and other material culture traits of Zion, Tuweap, the Moapa Valley, and Muddy Valley are not homogeneous. Differences between the ceramic complex of the Johnson-Paria district and the rest of the Virgin Kayenta region were once regarded sufficient by Colton to set these drainages apart within the larger Virgin context. Recently, however, these differences have been viewed as insignificant (Aikens 1965, p. 7). Stylistic variations within Virgin Kayenta rock art can also be distinguished and tentatively defined, and changes in the pattern of the rock-art record as one traces it from east to west correlate with changes in other archaeological data. Although the cultural developments in the Johnson-Paria section are recognized as being strongly similar to those in the Zion district, the closer association of the former with the Tsegi district has been noted (Schroeder 1955, p. 22) and this relationship is reflected in the San Juan Kayenta aspects of the rock art from this area. The dropping of certain eastern representational elements in the Nevada panels, as well as the weakening of certain Puebloan stylistic features such as the contained angular form, appears to correlate with the lack of other strongly Puebloan features in this peripheral region, such as the kiva and black-on-white painted pottery, and with the simplification of the black-on-gray pottery designs (Shutler 1961, pp. 66–67).

At this point, the discussion of the Virgin Kayenta rock art is fraught with numerous difficulties. Primarily the area lacks adequate coverage and therefore it is impossible to reconstruct with confidence a picture of the various stylistic fluctuations and their real distribution. The Arizona portion of the Virgin area, for example, is almost a complete blank, with a single site or record. Secondly, with the exception of the Nevada sites, the bulk of the documentation comes from a collection of previously published work, rather than from an original collection in the files. Most heavily drawn upon are the works by Judd (1926), Steward (1941), Rudy and Stirland (1950), Wauer (1965), and Schroeder (1955). Because of the use of secondary sources in which complete panels are only occasionally reproduced, it is difficult at times to obtain a feeling for a whole style and the relationships of the component elements.

In spite of these difficulties, the stylistic patterns that emerge from the available information tend to follow geographic lines, although there is a certain amount of overlap in the central part of the Virgin Kayenta area. Sites have been divided roughly into an eastern Virgin Kayenta Style and a western Virgin Kayenta Style, both of which are relatable in varying degrees to the Pueblo rock art in the Kayenta heartland east of the Virgin Kayenta region. In addition, there emerges in the central part of the Virgin Kayenta territory a rock art style, herein called the Cave Valley Style, which is distinguished by the presence of an anthropomorphic figure composed largely of triangular forms. Finally, one painted panel of Basketmaker II type paintings has been recorded from near Kanab.

A BASKETMAKER PAINTING FROM COTTONWOOD WASH, KANAB

A single Basketmaker II style painting is on record from the Virgin Kayenta region (Judd 1926, pp. 121–122, fig. 32). The painting, from Cottonwood Canyon near Kanab, consists of two or more anthropomorphs with elongated rectilinear or trapezoidal torsos (fig. 116). The body area of the largest figure is broad and decorated with a textile type of design. No excavations were undertaken in the cave in which this painting occurs, and its attribution to a Basketmaker II origin is made on the basis of its resemblances to Basketmaker paintings in the San Juan province. The figures, however, are also somewhat similar to the Barrier Canyon Style anthropomorphs in eastern Utah.

Judd (1926, p. 92) also mentions seeing "characteristic Basketmaker paintings" in Cave I in Cottonwood Canyon, and mentions these paintings in reference to illustrations of the triangular-bodied anthropomorphs typical of the Cave Valley Style (1926, p. 95, and pl. 60). These anthropomorphs, however, are believed to date from a more recent phase of Virgin Kayenta development. (See below.)

THE EASTERN VIRGIN KAYENTA STYLE

Petroglyphs in the Eastern Virgin Kayenta Style have been recorded primarily from the Johnson-Paria district by Steward (1941, figs. 57–58 and pls. 46–48) and Young (1929, p. 124). Steward illustrates three sites from Molly's Nipple Canyon, three from Oak Canyon, two from in and near Johnson Canyon, and one each from Wildcat and near Clark Canyons (fig. 115). These panels, exhibiting a proliferation of elements and emphasizing clear geometric designs and right angle forms, closely resemble petroglyph panels from the Kayenta area proper (figs. 117–121). With the

exception of the presence of a few insects and Cave Valley type anthropomorphs (see below), these panels are virtually indistinguishable from Style 4 Kayenta sites in Glen Canyon as defined by Turner (1963, pp. 6–7). Turner dates the Glen Canyon Style 4 between A.D. 1050 and 1250. He describes the material as follows (1963, p. 7):

The Style 4 diagnostic designs are: birds, flute players, hunting scenes, anthropomorphs with enlarged appendages and genitals, bird-bodied open-mouthed cloven sheep, concentric circles, and watchspring scrolls. Also included are the triangular-bodied elab-

FIGURE 116 Painted figures of Basketmaker type, Cottonwood Canyon, near Kanab. Source: Judd 1926, fig. 32.

FIGURE 117 Petroglyphs, Eastern Virgin Kayenta Style, Molly's Nipple Canyon. This panel is ten feet in width. Source: Steward 1941, fig. 57 e.

FIGURE 118 Mountain sheep and bow, Eastern Virgin Kayenta Style, Clark Canyon. Source: Steward 1941, fig. 63 h.

FIGURE 119 White painted geometric designs, Eastern Virgin Kayenta Style, Wild Cat Canyon. Source: Steward 1941, fig. 58 f, g, k.

FIGURE 120 Petroglyphs near Johnson Canyon, Site 11, Eastern Virgin Kayenta Style. Source: Steward 1941, fig. 60 f.

orately-headdressed anthropomorphs (Fig. 13). Dints [the mark or pit resulting from a single blow] are generally spaced equidistantly and the pecking technique was usually a well controlled hammerstone-chisel method. Design elaboration is rampant, with some scenes often having a humorous bent (Fig. 14). . . . Curvilinear and rectilinear designs and elements are also diagnostic.

Of singular importance in this style is the interest in right-angle forms in both abstract and representational elements. Anthropomorphic and lizard representations, for example, are usually built around this motif. Arms and legs are shown leaving the body at right angles and repeat the right-angle motif again at the joints.

It is possible that if more data were available from both the eastern Virgin Kayenta and the Glen Canyon regions, a detailed comparison might reveal distinguishing characteristics, particularly in the way of a figure type or element inventory.

The Glen Canyon region immediately to the east of the Johnson-Paria district also had a small Virgin Kayenta occupation (Gunnerson 1959b, p. 7, and Lister 1959a, p. 103) in addition to scattered groups of eastern Kayenta people. The rock art, as one would expect, is consistent with the Glen Canyon Style 4 elsewhere and no specifically Virgin characteristics have been observed (Scott file data: Foster 1954, figs. 12 and 15; Lister 1959a; Gunnerson, 1959b, figs. 14 and p. 43).

FIGURE 121 Petroglyphs, Eastern Virgin Kayenta Style, Site 30, Oak Canyon. Panel is nearly twenty feet in width. Large quadrupeds in upper left contrast typologically with other figures and may have a separate origin. Source: Steward 1941, pl. 48, top.

THE CAVE VALLEY STYLE

In the central part of the Virgin Kayenta area from Johnson Canyon to the western edge of Zion National Park (fig. 115) there are a number of sites which display a complex of figures readily distinguishable from the Eastern Virgin Kayenta Style. The name Cave Valley Style is suggested here as a designation for this development after the Cave Valley site 42Ws69 on the Kolob Plateau in Zion National Park in which the best examples of this style have been recorded to date (Rudy and Stirland 1950, figs. 5 d–f; and Wauer, 1965). The style has not been recognized as an entity by previous investigators, and although Wauer devotes a monograph to these paintings, he fails to relate them to similar figures at other rock art sites in the same general region. Nevertheless, other sites displaying Cave Valley Style figures as a group or occasionally in association with Eastern Virgin Kayenta Style panels are illustrated in the Scott files as well as in the published literature (Steward 1929, fig. 85 r and pl. 86 d; 1941, figs. 61 and 62 and pl. 48; Schroeder 1955, fig. 19 b and pl. 13 a and b; Judd 1926, pl. 60; and Mallery 1893, fig. 86).

Because of the lack of copious data the Cave Valley Style as described here is subject to future modification when more material has been collected. The style is characterized by the presence

of a highly stylized anthropomorphic figure to be described in detail below. All figures occurring in the style tend to be simple with few elaborations. The aesthetic quality of line is not developed and complex decorative detail is lacking (figs. 122–125). Cave Valley Style panels occur most commonly as paintings, although carved anthropomorphs of the Cave Valley type have been reported (Schroeder 1955, fig. 19 b). The paintings display a wide range of colors including black, red, yellow, green, pink, and white (Wauer 1965, p. 68, and Schroeder 1955, p. 89).

The Cave Valley Style anthropomorph may be larger than and somewhat dominant over the other figures in a given panel. In spite of having a triangular or tapering torso, this figure has characteristically a rather pudgy appearance. Arms and legs are generally short and may occur as thick lines or be triangular in form. The depiction of the legs, which often extend at right angles from the body base, resembles the basal element noted above on western Fremont anthropomorphs. Fingers and toes are shown in only a few instances, usually being absent altogether. Heads vary in shape from bucketlike to triangular or round. Horns have been reported on some figures although a decorative crown of vertically or horizontally aligned dots is a more usual form

FIGURE 122 Cave Valley Style painting, Cave Valley (42Ws69). Source: Wauer 1965, fig. 3 (mislabeled 4).

of headdress. In some cases a triangular or bucket-shaped head is shown with a flat extension across the top that is terminated with downward pointing projections which echo the larger design of the torso and its appendages. These variations among the Cave Valley type anthropomorphs may be seen in figures 122–124.

The Cave Valley Style anthropomorph is commonly found in association with smaller elements painted in the same blunt manner. These elements include other human figures, which may be depicted as crude stick forms painted in wide lines and may bear dot crown headdresses like those seen on the large triangular figure. A number of anthropomorphs are shown in profile, including flute players, phallic figures, people running, or lines of stick figures shown with arms outstretched in front of them (figs. 122, 124 b, e, f, and g, 125). Simple and unidentifiable animals associated with this style are usually rather formless and amoebalike in appearance (fig. 124 e and f). The usual abstract elements occurring in Cave Valley Style panels are rows of dots, short lines, v's, simple equilinear crosses, concentric circles, swastikas, wavy lines, and possibly handprints.

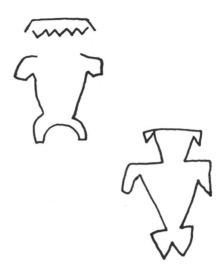

FIGURE 123 Cave Valley Style anthropomorphs, Cave Valley (42Ws69). Source: Rudy and Stirland 1950, fig. 5.

THE WESTERN VIRGIN KAYENTA STYLE

Two petroglyph sites described by Rudy and Stirland from Washington County in western Utah (1950, pp. 18 and 59–60) and several other sites from the lower Moapa Valley in southeastern Nevada form the basis for the Western Virgin Kayenta Style as defined here (fig. 115). It is possible that with additional data further stylistic divisions could be made, but on the basis of so few sites, stylistic splitting is currently unwarranted. Most of the Puebloan Nevada sites recorded in the Scott files have been previously discussed by Heizer and Baumhoff (1962, pp. 28–35), and have been included by these authors in the broader category of Great Basin Representational Style (which, as pointed out earlier, includes stylistically diverse material). Listings of all previous references to the Nevada sites can be found in their text and will not be reiterated here.

The rock art of the western Virgin Kayenta region consists largely of petroglyph panels of small, solidly carved representational figures and abstract elements. An interesting combination of elements showing Eastern Virgin Kayenta Style influences together with anthropomorphic figures

reflecting certain Cave Valley Style traits appears, although a number of characteristic features of the eastern Virgin Kayenta Style have dropped. There is a noticeable reduction in subject matter; hunting scenes, stick-figure lizards, and flute players appear less commonly, and there is a complete lack of Puebloan pottery designs and other strongly angular forms found in the eastern Virgin Kayenta sites nearer the Pueblo heartland. The Nevada panels, however, manifest new elements, some of which are due to the influence of the Great Basin abstract styles which begin to appear in this region and some of which are peculiar to the Western Virgin Kayenta Style.

Pueblo sites in Washington County, Utah, are described by Rudy and Stirland (1950, p. 59) as displaying sheep, deer, snakes, birds, horned toads, insects, scorpions, and human figures including hunters. Human figures are described as varying from being complete and engaged in various activities to static torsos. Complex circles, lines, dots, networks of lines, and animal tracks are also noted. Plate II, B–F (Rudy and Stirland 1950) illustrates, with a number of rather poor

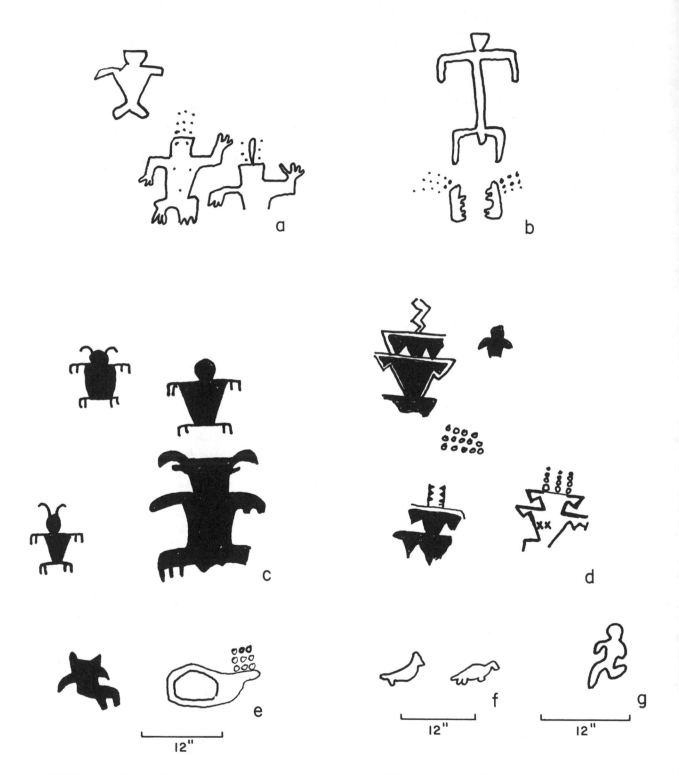

FIGURE 124 Cave Valley Style figures: a and b, Cave Valley (42Ws69) (Wauer 1965, fig. 4); c, Johnson Canyon (Steward 1941, fig. 61 a); d–f, Cottonwood Canyon, (Judd 1926, pl. 60).

FIGURE 125 Cave Valley Style paintings, Zion National Park. Source: postcard, Scott files.

FIGURE 126 Cave Valley Style anthropomorph, lizards, and miscellaneous other designs, Pipe Spring National Monument, Arizona. Source: Mallery 1893, fig. 86.

photographs, panels at 42Ws83 and 42Ws99. These display rather crudely carved human figures with tapering bodies and short hunched arms. Mountain sheep with long sweeping horns, and deer, as well as unidentifiable quadrupeds, are visible. The rounded silhouettes and lack of geometric designs and technical precision in carving distinguish these panels from Pueblo work farther east.

Documented Nevada sites are primarily from the Valley of Fire, Kane Springs, Mouse's Tank, and Lost City (figs. 127–131 and pls. 53–55). Representational elements present in these panels are various types of anthropomorphic figures, quadrupeds, largely mountain sheep and a rare deer, lizards, and hand- and footprints. Mountain sheep are depicted with crescent-shaped, rounded, rectangular, or thickened linear bodies, no type seeming to have preference or particular significance. Long canes or hooked vertical lines and atlatls are seen for the first time. Grant (1968, p. 124) ascribes the presence of atlatls and stirrup-shaped objects resembling Coso "Medicine bags" at one Valley of Fire site as due to western Shoshonean influence. Another development is the anthropomorph with highly exaggerated fingers and toes (fig. 127 and pl. 53). The human form is often rendered as a stick figure and may be phallic. Arms are usually held out straight or slightly hunched and curved downward. A further abstraction on this theme is found in several designs consisting of a vertical body stem crossed with numerous hooked or downward curving lines (figs. 128 and pl. 54). Some anthropomorphs are depicted with rectangular or more rarely with triangular bodies. Horns or heads with flat crown and downward pointing corner projections resemble features of the Cave Valley Style anthropomorphs (fig. 129). The human figure is rarely shown pursuing any kind of activity, an exception to this being the hand-holding groups from Mouse's Tank (CI–145) (Heizer and Baumhoff 1962, figs. 69 c, 70 a, and 76 a).

In addition to the usual spiral, dot row, and concentric circles and wavy lines appearing in most Virgin Kayenta sites, abstract designs characteristic of the Great Basin Rectilinear and Curvilinear Styles occur in panels with the representative elements and appear to be contemporary (figs. 130–131). Among these elements are rakes, joined circles, sets of parallel lines, two-pole ladders, lunettes suspended from a base line, segmented concentric circles, and a number of undescribable figures. At Atlatl Rock in the Valley of Fire near Overton, Western Virgin Kayenta Style representative elements include anthropomorphs, mountain sheep, fat footprints, and atlatls, as well as certain abstract designs, and are superimposed over a complex of more weathered abstract motifs. This panel is discussed by Steward as follows (1929, p. 147 and pl. 72):

FIGURE 127 Petroglyphs, Western Virgin Kayenta Style, Kane Springs, Nevada, Cl–4. Source: Schellbach photo.

PLATE 53 Petroglyphs, Western Virgin Kayenta Style, Lost City Site, Nevada, Cl–5. Louis Schellbach photo.

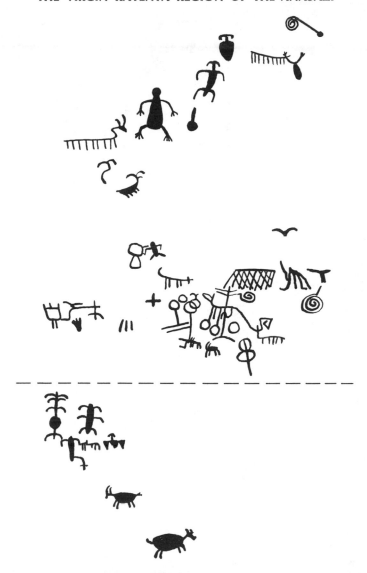

FIGURE 128   Petroglyphs, Western Virgin Kayenta Style, The Lost City Site, Valley of Fire, Nevada, Cl–5. Source: Schellbach photo.

Plate 72 shows several mountain sheep. In the lower lefthand corner of the photographs are several rectilinear designs which recall those found at Grapevine Canyon in southwestern [southeastern] Nevada. Among these are two "gridirons" of the type found in Owens valley, notably near Bishop and as far north as Virginia City, Nevada. In this group we also find a series of circles connected by straight lines, typical of the northern desert region. Concentric circles and "spoked wheels" also appear. Wavy lines and various indefinable curvilinear designs are abundant. Many of these designs have been put over older designs, some of which are very indefinite. Whether this unclearness is due to the underlying designs being less deeply carved than the more recent cannot be determined, but

they give the appearance of considerable weathering Among those designs which stand out more sharply none are essentially different from the older ones except the spoked wheels and concentric circles which appear in only clear-cut designs, completely hiding the figures under them.

Steward does not make it clear whether or not the mountain sheep and other representational elements are present in the underlying complex, but none appear to be in the photographs. As pointed out by Heizer and Baumhoff (1962, p. 30), Steward was mistaken in attributing his plate 72 to Lost City rather than to Atlatl Rock.

FIGURE 129   Rock paintings in red, green, and purple, Western Virgin Kayenta Style. Lost City Site, Valley of Fire, Nevada, Cl-5. Source: Schellbach photo.

FIGURE 130   Petroglyphs, Western Virgin Kayenta Style, Atlatl Rock, Valley of Fire, Nevada, Cl-1. Source: M. R. Harrington photo.

PLATE 54   Petroglyphs, Western Virgin Kayenta Style, Lost City, Nevada, Cl–5. Louis Schellbach photo.

FIGURE 131 Petroglyphs, Western Virgin Kayenta Style, a partial reconstruction; Atlatl Rock, Valley of Fire, Nevada, Cl–1. Source: M. R. Harrington photo.

PLATE 55 Petroglyphs, Western Virgin Kayenta Style, Atlatl Rock, Valley of Fire, Nevada, Cl–1. Louis Schellbach photo.

VII

Chronology

DATING THE VIRGIN KAYENTA STYLES

With the exception of the Cave Valley site paintings, Virgin Kayenta rock art has never been made a study in itself, and the data available have been recorded in conjunction with large site surveys or for popular interest; no specific effort has been made to date this art. Nevertheless, certain inferences can be made about the age of the Eastern and Western Virgin Kayenta Styles on the basis of what is known about related developments in the eastern Kayenta area. Also, in conjunction with discussing possible dates for the styles occurring within the Virgin Kayenta region, the chronological development of the Virgin Kayenta culture as a whole should be reviewed. The chronological scheme recently proposed as a tentative hypothesis by Ambler (1969, p. 113) reads as follows:

Although a few Basketmaker II and more Basketmaker III sites have been discovered in the Virgin area, they may be much later than their counterparts in the heart of the Anasazi are, judging by the facts that Basketmaker II may have lasted until after A.D. 700 in the Navajo Mountain area, implying that in still more marginal situations it would have been even later; and there is no evidence of a Pueblo I Period in the Virgin area analogous to the San Juan Pueblo I period (Schroeder 1955: 13). Thus Basketmaker III in the Virgin area may have lasted until about A.D. 1000, when the expansion of Pueblo II cultural development reached the area, resulting in the indistinct temporal line between the end of Basketmaker and the beginning of Pueblo development in the area and the presence of Basketmaker traits at Pueblo period sites in the area.

Following this line of reasoning, we could date the Basketmaker style paintings from Cottonwood Canyon near Kanab as late as A.D. 700 or even later, although a date several centuries earlier is also possible. Cave du Pont, the well-known Basketmaker II site in the Kanab vicinity, has long been thought to be securely dated by one tree-ring specimen at A.D. 217, but the Laboratory of Tree-Ring Research now considers that "the nature of the cross-dating does not conform to pres-

ent standards and the date must be discarded." (Bannister, Dean, and Robinson 1969, p. 11.) This, of course, does not imply that anything in the tree-ring evidence militates *against* an early date. The strongly Puebloan Eastern and Western Virgin Kayenta Styles probably date between A.D. 1000, when the Pueblo II cultural development reached the area, and the end of the Virgin Kayenta development sometime in the 12th century. Suggested terminal dates for the Virgin Kayenta culture vary within a hundred year period. The situation as summarized by Ambler (1969, p. 113) is as follows:

Aikens (1965) places the end of the Virgin development at A.D. 1200, apparently on the basis of the presence of three sherds of Flagstaff Black-on-white at Bonanza Dune. Since Flagstaff Black-on-white started at least as early as 1100 (Breternitz 1966), I would suggest that an earlier date is possible. Shutler (1961: 69) suggests a date of 1150 for the end of the last period of Pueblo occupation in southern Nevada, apparently based on the presence of Citadel Polychrome. Since Citadel Polychrome also apparently started about 1100 (Breternitz 1966; Ambler, Lindsay, and Stein 1964: 77), even that could be too late. I would therefore suggest the possibility that the Virgin development came to an end between 1100 and 1125.

It should be noted that the Glen Canyon Style 4 petroglyphs, which appear to be essentially identical with the Eastern Virgin Kayenta stylistic manifestation, are dated between A.D. 1050 and 1250 on the basis of petroglyph-pottery associations (Turner 1963, p. 12). This time span correlates generally with the proposed dates for the Virgin Kayenta development. Nevertheless, an earlier termination date for the Eastern and Western Virgin Kayenta Styles, perhaps by as much as one hundred years, is possible.

Dates for the Cave Valley Style paintings are less easily postulated. Although paintings at the Cave Valley site on the Kolob Plateau were studied in detail, few temporal data emerged (Wauer, 1965). Wauer suggests that possibly two ages of paintings are represented at this site, because the brighter colored paintings are superimposed over black figures; nevertheless, no stylistic changes could be discerned between the two layers (1965, p. 67). No excavations were made at the site. According to Rudy and Stirland (1950, p. 18), other than the rock art itself, there is little evidence of occupation in the cave.

Unfortunately, the individuality of the Cave Valley Style as a whole prevents a comparison between it and datable styles in other Pueblo areas. At the most, one can postulate that the Cave Valley Style is representative of one phase of Virgin Kayenta work which centered geographically in the region of Zion. A post-Basketmaker II date for this style is suggested.

THE AGE OF FREMONT ROCK ART

At this point, without any direct methods of dating rock paintings and carvings themselves, the business of dating Fremont rock art depends largely on dating the Fremont culture. Temporal control in Fremont research has been somewhat inadequate, and a wide variety of opinions regarding Fremont dating still prevails.

In an evaluation of the available tree-ring, Carbon-14, and ceramic evidence, Ambler (1969, p. 107) concluded that the entire Fremont manifestation in Utah could be generally confined to the period between A.D. 1050 and 1200. Among the possible dating mechanisms, Ambler feels that the most reliable is the study of the occurrences of Anasazi pottery in Fremont sites and vice versa. He says (1969, pp. 109–110), "At no Fremont site have any pottery types ever been found whose temporal range is stated as ending prior to 1050, nor have any types been found that commence after 1200. Conversely, no Fremont pottery has been found at Anasazi sites containing only pre-1050 or post-1200 materials." However, more recently, on the basis of additional evidence provided by radiocarbon dating, he has expanded the time range allowable for the Fremont culture by fifty years, thus suggesting the time between A.D. 1000 and 1200 for its duration (Ambler, 1970).

It is notable that the majority of the tree-ring dates obtained by Schulman (1948 and 1951) and Ferguson (1949) from sites in Nine Mile and Hill Canyons cluster around A.D. 1200, thus substantiating the ceramic evidence cited by Ambler. In another recent review of Fremont dates, Gunnerson concludes: "When all the evidence is considered together the span of the Fremont Culture cannot be compressed to include any less than the period ca. A.D. 950–1150, and the later date could more reasonably be placed significantly later, at least as late as A.D. 1200. There is less to suggest that the beginning of Fremont was earlier than A.D. 950, although it is always possible that additional work may produce a series of

datable beams that will extend the scope of Fremont in that direction" (1969, p. 70). Gunnerson is thus in substantial agreement with Ambler except that he thinks there is evidence for a beginning date not less than fifty years earlier than Ambler thinks is established; a difference that will not be of critical importance to the discussion of the origin and relationships of Fremont rock art which follows here.

It should be pointed out, however, that the date of A.D. 950 cited by Gunnerson is derived from a tree-ring date which may or may not be reliable by itself. Early tree-ring dates may result from a likely time gap between the death of a tree and its use. Also the outermost rings on many specimens may be missing, and thus the latest years of a tree's growth may be unaccounted for. Taking these factors into consideration, the single tree-ring date of A.D. 750 from Marigold Cave in Castle Park on the Yampa River in northwestern Colorado is regarded as highly tentative, especially in the absence of dated companion beams (Schulman 1950, p. 18, and Gunnerson 1969, p. 168).

Still earlier beginning dates of A.D. 400–500 for the Fremont culture in Colorado have been proposed for the Yampa River sites by Burgh and Scoggin (1948), and these dates have been accepted and quoted by subsequent scholars (Lister 1951, p. 46; Jennings and others 1956, pp. 102–103; and Taylor 1957, pp. 146–147). These dates, however, were originally estimated on the basis of the general resemblance of some of the Fremont materials to Basketmaker III material in the Anasazi without any allowance for the time involved for the diffusion of these traits and are now thus regarded with skepticism (Ambler 1966a, pp. 262–263). More recently, a beginning date of A.D. 600 for the Fremont occupation of the Uinta Basin has been proposed by Shields (1970) on the basis of C–14 and tree-ring dates, while Fry (1970) and Aikens (1970) suggest that the Fremont culture in the Salt Lake region begins as early as A.D. 400. The early date in regard to the

Uinta Basin has been rejected by Breternitz (1970), who is in substantial agreement with Ambler.

A later terminal date for the Fremont culture than that postulated above by Ambler, Gunnerson, and Breternitz might be suggested by a small number of Carbon-14 dates which fall outside the norm (Crane and Griffin 1958, p. 1121; Sharrock and Marwitt 1967, p. 51; and Aikens 1966b, p. 14). Most of these late dates, however, for various reasons have been rejected as unreliable (Ambler 1969, pp. 108–109). A possible exception to this are the 1350±90 and 1650±100 dates obtained by Aikens at the Injun Creek site in the Salt Lake region. These dates are accepted by Aikens, but their validity remains to be affirmed. Without more evidence to support the reliability of these dates, or if they are valid, to support their appli-

cability for the remainder of the Fremont area, it is assumed that the earlier terminal dates suggested above are relevant to the bulk of the Fremont rock art under consideration in this paper.

In conclusion then, since much of the current data suggests that the cultural configuration recognizable as Fremont dates largely between A.D. 1000 (give or take 50 years) and 1200, it is assumed at this time that most of the Fremont rock art falls within this period. Exceptions to this statement are most likely to occur in the northern Fremont regions of Great Salt Lake and the Uinta Basin, where earlier dates have been proposed by certain investigators. Readers desiring more information on the details of Fremont chronology are referred to Ambler (1969), Gunnerson (1969, pp. 167–170), and Breternitz (1970) for discussion of the current data and the problems therein.

EVIDENCE FOR CHRONOLOGICAL DEVELOPMENT IN FREMONT ROCK ART

Areal variation within the Fremont rock art tradition has been clearly demonstrated in the descriptive section of this paper. Whether or not temporal variation is demonstrable is not yet obvious. A great deal more closely datable material must be gathered from specific sites with associated rock art panels before temporal variations within Fremont rock art can be perceived with any certainty.

There is some suggestion that a certain amount of development within the tradition may be in evidence from superimpositions, but again our data in this regard are extraordinarily meager. Of some interest in this connection, however, are the anthropomorphs described above from the Vernal-Dinosaur district in the Uintah Fremont region which are defined by means of closely spaced holes. According to Reagan's notes on file with the Museum of New Mexico, these carvings appear to be the oldest in the panels where they occur, since more conventional Fremont designs are superimposed over them. If Reagan is right, then the ornate anthropomorphic figure would appear to be present early in the eastern Fremont development. However, other chronological schemes suggested by Reagan are unconvincing and contradictory and seem to be grounded more on fanciful conjecture than on real evidence.

An instance of superimpositions with stylistic changes is the sequence in the Thompson panel in the southern San Rafael zone described earlier (p. 42). Morss suggests that the sequence of superimpositions of the three types of anthro-

pomorphs represents three distinct periods illustrating the development of Fremont art from Basketmaker or quasi-Basketmaker prototypes (1931, p. 39). In other southern San Rafael panels, however, plain solidly pecked anthropomorphs and ornamented outline figures appear to be contemporary. It is conceivable that after their development all types persisted and continued to be made contemporaneously. At best, one can only conclude that currently panels cannot be assigned a relative position in Fremont rock art development on the basis of the presence of certain anthropomorphic types. Nevertheless, the variation among the southern San Rafael anthropomorphs does suggest that temporal as well as geographic factors may be involved.

One argument for the probable occurrence of the ornate treatment of the anthropomorphic figure relatively early in the development of Fremont rock art may be based on the Pillings figurines from Range Creek and similar figurines reported from the Old Woman site by Taylor (1957, pp. 40–46, figs. 19–21). These figurines closely resemble certain complex anthropomorphic petroglyph figure types from both the Vernal-Dinosaur district and the southern San Rafael region, particularly in details of the head, necklace, waist, and kilt. Michigan radio-carbon dates from the Old Woman site were 780±250 and 890±200 (Crane and Griffin 1959, p. 189). (Note: the date listed in Crane and Griffin as pertaining to the Poplar Knob site was judged by Ambler (1969, p. 108) to be an Old Woman site date.) Ambler

(1969, p. 108) regards the center dates as "perhaps a bit early" and the upper sigma deviation as being more nearly correct for the site. It should be pointed out that a time gap between the death and the use of the wood may account for early resulting dates, as in dendrochronology. The Pillings figurines have been dated from the 11th century (Morss 1954, p. 25). It is highly likely that this complex concept of the human figure would have been applied contemporaneously to the figurines and to the rock carvings alike.

One other attempt has been made to discern a developmental pattern in Fremont rock art. In the La Sal Mountains of southeastern Utah, Hunt (1953) made a study of numerous petroglyphs and rock paintings of both Pueblo and Fremont origin. As a result of her research, she suggests traits characteristic of early and late Fremont rock art in the area. According to Hunt the early sites are distinguished by large triangular painted figures and trapezoidal horned anthropomorphs. From "late" sites she describes ornamented figures, men with shields, and flute players (1953, p. 20). It is my feeling that these chronological distinctions need more supportive evidence to be convincing. Furthermore, she indicates that, in general, the "early" Fremont complex in the La Sal Mountains resembles that of the Fremont River district and Castle Park in Colorado, and the "late" Fremont configuration is more akin to the Fremont manifestations in Nine Mile Canyon, resemblances which are not particularly well borne out.

THE AGE AND CULTURAL AFFILIATIONS OF THE BARRIER CANYON STYLE PAINTINGS

The Barrier Canyon Style paintings pose several problems which are difficult to answer at this time. The sites are in the eastern part of the southern San Rafael region, a fact which presents the obvious question of whether or not they are a local Fremont development. Lacking adequate archaeological data pertaining to the age and cultural affiliations of these paintings, I will attempt certain arm-chair evaluations on the basis of available evidence. In order to accomplish this, it is necessary to do four things: (1) review and evaluate the scant archaeological findings of previous investigators, (2) assess the evidence present in the paintings themselves, (3) review the few superimpositions that do occur, and (4) make a stylistic comparison with other rock art styles which might give clues to the horizontal and vertical cultural relationships of the Barrier Canyon Style.

ARCHAEOLOGICAL EVIDENCE

Unfortunately the archaeology of these sites has been very little studied and, with a single exception, those observations that have been made are of a relatively superficial nature, usually in connection with large scale site surveys. In the vicinity of Thompson Wash, where both Barrier Canyon Style paintings and Fremont petroglyphs occur, there is very little evidence of occupation (Gunnerson 1957, p. 73). Slightly more data are available from Barrier Canyon and the North Wash (Crescent Creek) rock shelter (Claflin-Emerson Expedition, Site H3-4, Gunnerson 1969, p. 36). The latter site is located about ten miles from the Colorado River, and the shelter is situated near the mouth of a side canyon which is well watered with permanent springs. A moccasin found in this shelter by the Claflin-Emerson Expedition was referred to by Morss (1931, p. 39) as Fremont, but according to Gunnerson (1969, p. 37) was not of the Fremont style, but resembles the Basketmaker II type described by Guernsey (1931, pp. 66–68). Birney (1933) mentions finding an arrow-shaft, a worked antler tip, a broken bone awl, and a digging stick fragment at this site, while Steward (1941, p. 329) describes the presence of corn cobs and twelve rooms of crude masonry put together without mortar. It would seem that perhaps more than one occupation is involved.

A number of archaeological sites in Barrier Canyon have been described by Malouf (1941). In his survey Malouf found that most of the archaeological material was located fifteen miles from the mouth at the only point at which the canyon could be traversed. Springs are also present at this point in the canyon. Large rock paintings were located two miles farther on. At the habitation sites he found that stone-walled structures were absent, but he mentions arrowhead types and pottery which he dates between A.D. 800 and 1300 (1941, p. 153). He believes that the habitation sites were largely hunting camps for parties coming from the Colorado and that the rock paintings and other cultural remains are contemporary. He is also of the opinion, however, that there are enough differences between many of the petroglyphs and rock paintings to warrant the conjecture that they represent different periods, but he does not carry this analysis further.

Of considerable interest in regard to Barrier Canyon is the one intensive excavation there by the Claflin-Emerson expedition, recently described by Gunnerson (1969, pp. 67–68). This excavation was carried out in Horseshoe Shelter (SR–12–5), the only painted site showing much evidence of occupation at all, for the express purpose of discovering the cultural affiliations of the paintings. The excavation, however, did not clarify this problem, as three occupational levels were revealed. The first was a preceramic level, above which a Fremont and a Mesa Verde occupation occurred. The latter two appear to have been mixed. In the light of the representational content of the Barrier Canyon Style paintings (see below) and their stylistic affiliations, however, the presence of a preceramic level at this site is noteworthy.

Field investigations of the physical locations of these panels might be of some value in age determination. From the photographs it appears that at least two and possibly three of the most extensive Barrier Canyon panels are situated high above the current ground level and consequently out of contemporary human reach. As mentioned earlier, the base of the Great Gallery figures are as much as from three to five meters above the shelter floor (Gunnerson 1969, p. 65). The base of the North Wash painting is located about ten feet above the present floor level of the shelter. Such height might suggest considerable antiquity for the paintings, in order to account for the removal of a former higher floor or ledge. Without comparative data, however, in regard to the situations of known Fremont panels or the locations of Barrier Canyon Style paintings in comparison with other rock art in the same shelter, a consideration of this factor is not particularly profitable at this time.

INTERNAL EVIDENCE IN THE PAINTINGS

In turning to the paintings themselves, we find only a small amount of internal evidence that might help in dating them. Because of the heavy emphasis on anthropomorphic representation, very few objects are portrayed in the paintings. It is of considerable interest that the bow and arrow, which is commonly represented in Fremont art, is absent in all recorded examples of the Barrier Canyon Style. In one instance, men are shown with spears (pl. 37). The earliest appearance of the bow and arrow in Utah and the Southwest has not been securely dated, although there seems to be a consensus (Wormington 1951, p. 55, and McGregor 1965, p. 213) that it first shows up in the San Juan drainage in the late Basketmaker III period some time between A.D. 650 and 700.

The splayed sticks and sickle-shaped objects in the Horse Canyon painting merit some comment. These tools are represented in a panel in which seeded grasses and other wild plants are also held in the hands of the anthropomorphic figures, and one may suggest from this association that the tools had to do with the collection of uncultivated plant food. Bundles of willow twigs lashed together at the base and spread at the tops are described and illustrated by Kidder and Guernsey from a Monument Valley cliff-house site (1919, pl. 48, p. 120). These writers express the opinion that such contrivances were used to knock seeds from grass plants into gathering baskets. It is worthy of note that the figure holding this tool may well be carrying such a basket instead of being hunchbacked. A sickle of mountain sheep horn has been reported from SR–12–5 in Barrier Canyon (Gunnerson 1969, p. 72). This is a site of mixed occupation and the cultural affiliations of the tool are not clear. Another sickle-shaped object comes from FL–12–5 on the Fremont River, (Morss 1931, p. 59, and Gunnerson 1969, p. 75). Sickle-shaped horn tools have also been found in southwestern sites (Kidder and Guernsey 1919, p. 128; Steward 1941, p. 317; and Adams and others 1961, p. 49), but their use seems to have been for abrading and scraping purposes. Neither the "seed-beater" nor the mountain sheep horn tool as it appears in southwestern sites has been closely dated. Both have been found in possibly Basketmaker contexts as well as associated with late Anasazi remains, the latter dating as late as the 13th century. This ambiguous cultural association of the horn tool in the Barrier Canyon site and the fact that both the "sickle' and the "seed-beater" appear to have had a long history of use in the Southwest render their representation in the Barrier Canyon Style paintings useless for dating purposes at the current time. Finally, the plant representations themselves are not necessarily a sound clue to the cultural affiliation and consequent age of the paintings, since the Fremont people, like the hunters and gatherers before them, were dependent on wild plants for a significant part of their food supply (Wormington 1955, p. 173).

SUPERIMPOSITIONS

Superimpositions of one style over the other have been mentioned in the course of site descriptions.

In no instance does a Barrier Canyon Style figure overlay one of recognized Fremont origin. The carved sheep in the Great Gallery in Barrier Canyon which underlay the painting are not of a type usually found in Fremont work. At Temple Mountain Wash a painting of a Fremont anthropomorph clearly overlays earlier and more faded Barrier Canyon Style work. This is perhaps the clearest instance of this phenomenon on record to date. However, at Moab and Thompson carved Fremont type quadrupeds overlay Barrier Canyon Style figures. At Fish Creek Cove Fremont type petroglyphs are superimposed over the animal paintings. Although these last are not exactly typical examples of the Barrier Canyon Style, there is some indication that they may have been done by Barrier Canyon Style artists. Thus, this line of evidence suggests that the Barrier Canyon Style preceded the Fremont in date.

STYLISTIC EVIDENCE

The stylistic relationship between the Barrier Canyon Style paintings and other rock art styles is of considerable interest, and although a comparative investigation along these lines produces no conclusive evidence as to cultural affiliations or age of these paintings, it is perhaps a productive route of exploration. A comparison between the Barrier Canyon Style and the eastern Fremont anthropomorphs has already been touched upon, and transitional figures have been described (pp. 79–82). When the total amount of available data is taken into consideration, however, it is apparent that the transitional figures are exceptional. Although gross similarities between certain of the eastern Fremont stylistic groupings, particularly in the southern San Rafael, and the Barrier Canyon Style paintings are obvious, further study suggests that the differences in detail as well as in overall aesthetic impact far outweigh the likenesses.

Similarities between the surrounding Fremont art and the Barrier Canyon Style paintings are found largely in certain general features, namely, in the predominance of the large anthropomorphic figure that is often characterized by a tapered body and an ample head which may be round, rectangular, or bucket-shaped. In both the Barrier Canyon Style and in the Fremont work, particularly in the southern San Rafael zone, there is a tendency to portray only the head and torso, leaving out the arms and legs. Snakes may occur in association with anthropomorphs in south San Rafael Fremont work as in the Barrier Canyon style. Further elaborations are abundant but generally differ significantly between the Barrier Can-

yon Style paintings and the Fremont work as table 7 indicates. The few other shared features between these two major stylistic groups are of relatively rare occurrences and their significance is questionable. They are pointed out here simply because of their specific nature. These shared features are (1) the occasional three-quarter view portrayal of the broad-shouldered human figure, (2) the depiction of a small vertical, or "pouch" animal, which occurs once in the Fremont material and three times in the Barrier Canyon Style paintings, (3) the occurrence once in each group of the dancing man and animal scene, and (4) arcs over the heads and over or through the bodies of human figures, a phenomenon occurring once in the Barrier Canyon Style paintings at Buckhorn, once in the Great Gallery, and in an occasional Fremont panel throughout the eastern Fremont area.

Beyond this the resemblances cease. The Barrier Canyon Style anthropomorphic figure departs from the Fremont depiction not only in form emphasis, but also in nearly every aspect of decorative detail. Also significant is the seemingly random arrangement of the relatively prolific numbers of quadrupeds and abstract elements appearing in Fremont panels contrasted with the compositional arrangement of a few small zoomorphs unified by the presence of a large anthropomorph, a repetitive theme in Barrier Canyon Style art. Abstract elements are extremely rare in the Barrier Canyon Style (fig. 7). Finally, the lack of any Anasazi impact upon the Barrier Canyon Style is notable. Comparisons between the Barrier Canyon Style and Fremont art are listed in table 7. In sum, it appears that the Barrier Canyon Style is a discrete entity, distinct from anything otherwise identifiable as Fremont.

Given this conclusion, we may then hypothesize that the Barrier Canyon Style paintings are not of Fremont origin, for if these paintings were indeed a local Fremont development it is likely that there would be a much higher number of shared traits than actually occurs. Furthermore, it should be pointed out that Barrier Canyon Style panels occur in the same localities as Fremont work as evidenced at Thompson Wash, Temple Mt. Wash, Ferron Creek east of Ferron, Short Canyon, Barrier Canyon. It is unlikely that both Southern San Rafael Fremont and Barrier Canyon Style art would have been executed at the same spot by the same peoples. The general similarities that do exist between the Fremont rock art and the Barrier Canyon Style paintings and the few actual transitional panels described earlier can be explained on other grounds. These phenomena could result from Fremont borrowing from a hypothetical contemporaneous ethnic group, or could be viewed in terms of evolutionary development. The possibility that the Barrier Canyon Style paintings predate the Fremont complex finds tentative support both in the Horseshoe Shelter excavations and in the superimpositions described earlier, as well as in a further stylistic comparison.

As strange as it may seem at first, certain rather significant parallels can be drawn between the Barrier Canyon Style of the Colorado River drainage and the Western Archaic Pecos River Style paintings in Texas. In contrast to the static, rather somber, and sometimes ghostly forms of the Barrier Canyon Style anthropomorphic figures, which compose the major part of any panel, the Pecos River Style anthropomorphs serve only as vertical notes in a complex composition united in flamboyant design by sinuous arcs and the sweeping lines of atlatls, fringed pouches flaring out on long strings, and a myriad of other objects, and superficially there seems to be little in the way of likeness between them. Closer examination reveals, however, that the majority of the features in the simpler Barrier Canyon Style paintings find counterparts among the complexities of the Pecos River Style. These are summarized in a comparative type chart (fig. 132). The elongate, tapering anthropomorphic figures, the dominant element in both styles, resemble one another in general shape as well as in some specific details. The acephalous nature of certain Barrier Canyon Style torsos, the bottle-shaped figures in the Great Gallery, and the short upcurving arms of the profile figure at Willow Tanks find parallels in the Pecos River Style panels (Newcomb 1967, pl. 15, and pl. 30, no. 4). Arms and legs, more commonly portrayed in the Texas art, may occur in both styles as short extensions of the shoulder or torso line respectively, and in many instances the arms tend to be uplifted. Decorative detail may vary between them, but rabbit-ear headgear and crowns defined by short lines and torso decoration consisting of interior panels, vertical center bands, striping, and wavy lines are all features shared by both groups. The vertical wavy line present at the sides of anthropomorphs in the Barrier Canyon Style find counterparts in the numerous sinuous lines at the sides or radiating from the shoulder region of numerous Pecos River Style anthropomorphs (Newcomb 1967, pls. 1; 8; 10; 19, no. 2; 27, no. 4; etc.). Other motifs flanking the anthropomorphic figure also occur in both styles.

Other Barrier Canyon Style elements in close association with the human figure, namely, the large quadruped with upcurved tail, and the tiny anthropomorphs, animals, and birds approaching the sides of the large anthropomorph or forming compositional arrangements nearby, and the depiction of wild plants are all present in the Pecos River Style paintings. The doglike figure with the curved-up tail finds its counterpart in the large cougar depictions present in a number of the Pecos River sites (Newcomb 1967, pls. 5; 24; 26; and 33, no. 1). Although small zoomorphs directly approaching an anthropomorph in a way similar to those in the Barrier Canyon panel SR–12–4a (fig. 75) and the Bird Site (fig. 76) are only occasional in the Pecos River art (Newcomb 1967, pls. 11, and 18, no. 9), compositional arrangements of these diminutive figures, including anthropomorphs, are quite common (Newcomb 1967, pls. 1; 2; 9, no. 1; 11, no. 2; and 13, no. 3). In addition, the groups of hunted deer occurring at the foot of anthropomorphic figures (Newcomb 1967, pls. 23; 25; and 28, no. 2) are reminiscent of the triangular arrangement of mountain sheep in the Great Gallery. Even the vertical "pouch" animal of the Barrier Canyon Style may have a Pecos River Style counterpart (Newcomb 1967, pl. 11), although the similarity here is less obvious.

Another feature present in one Barrier Canyon Style site is the arc seen in the Buckhorn Wash panel. This element was previously noted in conjunction with the Fremont material, particularly in the Vernal district sites. Similar arcs also occur in the Pecos River paintings, although in the latter instance they are frequently in the form of wavy lines (Newcomb 1967, pls. 12, no. 2; 17, no. 6; and 39, no. 1).

The wealth of additional elements present in the Pecos River Style paintings but absent in the Barrier Canyon Style, such as the fringed torsos of the anthropomorphs, atlatls, darts, rabbit sticks, and fringed pouches, as well as a large number of elements which defy description, are of less significance to the current discussion than is the observation that the aspects of the Barrier Canyon Style paintings lacking counterparts in the Pecos River Style are relatively few. These include the type of torso decoration involving horizontal decorative bands further embellished with small white dots or scratched lines simulating textile designs, and the dot decoration of the face and crown. Short antennalike headdresses, earrings, and striped neck decoration are also lacking in the Pecos River Style anthropomorphic design, as are facial features of any sort. The ghostlike

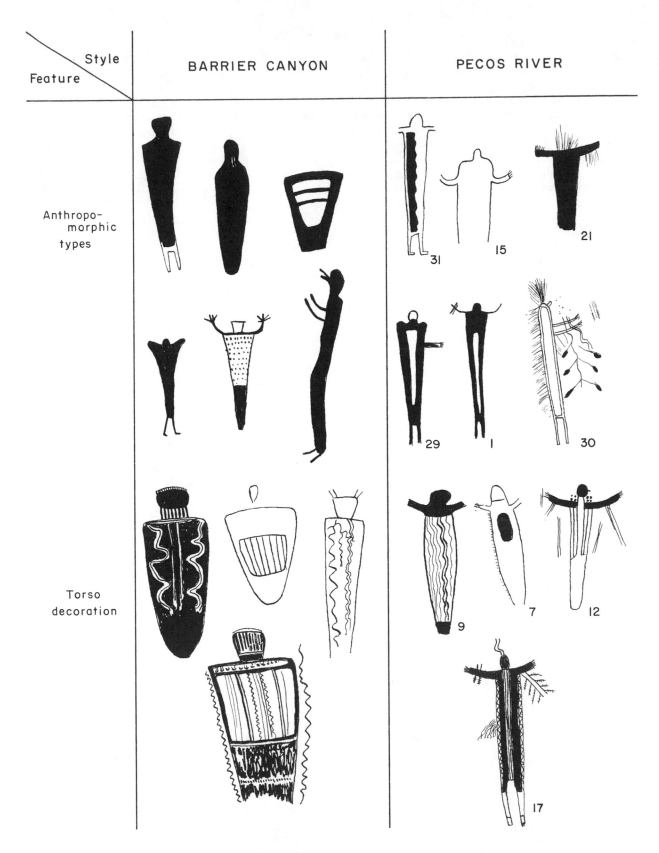

FIGURE 132 Chart comparing points of similarity between the Barrier Canyon and Pecos River Styles. Number accompanying the Pecos River Style figures refers to the plate reference in Newcomb 1967.

	BARRIER CANYON	PECOS RIVER
Style / Feature		

Wavy lines at sides of anthropomorphic figures		
Quadruped with curved-up tail		
Small zoomorphs approaching anthropomorphic figures		
Wild plants held by anthropomorphs		

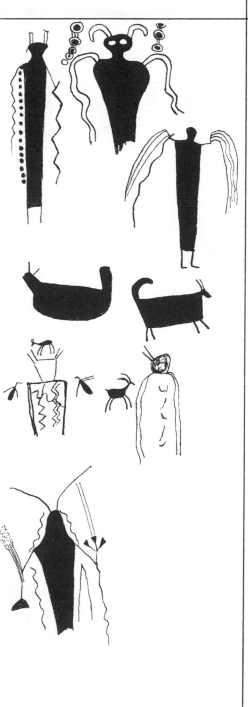
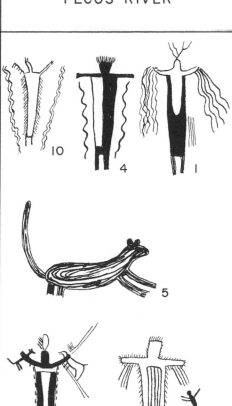
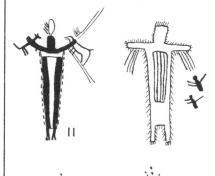
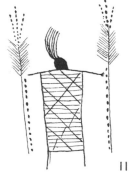

FIGURE 132 (continued)

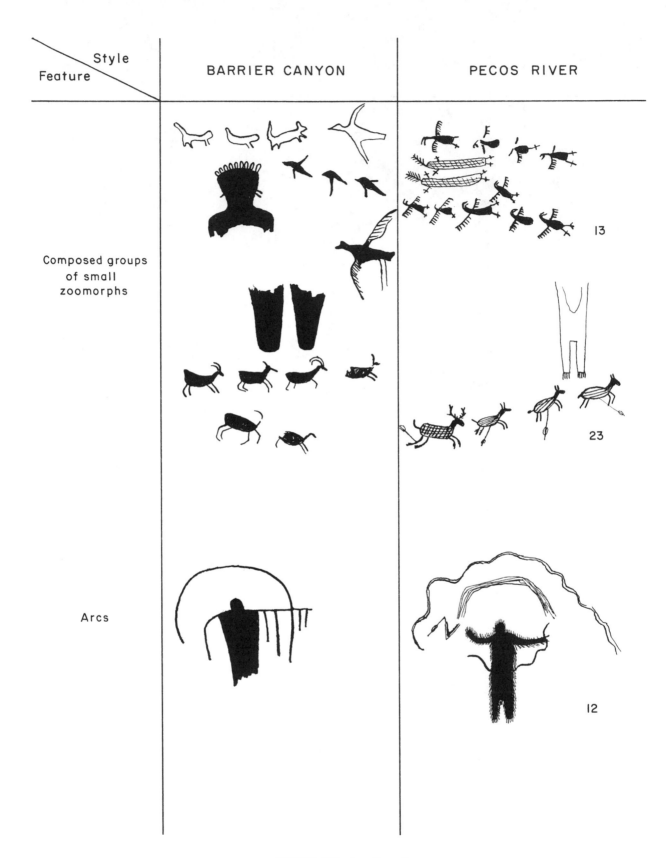

Style\Feature	BARRIER CANYON	PECOS RIVER
Composed groups of small zoomorphs		13
		23
Arcs		12

FIGURE 132 (continued)

aspect of Barrier Canyon Style figures is absent in the Texas art.

It should be stressed that many of the resemblances between the two styles are rather specific. This brings us back to our original consideration of whether or not a comparison of styles could lend any clue as to the age and cultural affiliations of the Barrier Canyon Style paintings. Although none of the evidence examined has been conclusive, the specific similarities between the Barrier Canyon Style and the Western Archaic Pecos River paintings support the possibility that the Barrier Canyon Style artists were indeed participants in a wide-ranging Western Archaic Period rock art tradition which was distinct from the Desert Culture rock art in the Great Basin.

The actual age of the Pecos River Style paintings has not been closely determined, although a four-period developmental sequence has been defined by Newcomb (1967). The Western Archaic remains in the Pecos River region have been dated between 6000 B.C. and A.D. 600, and although the association of the paintings with these remains is well established, no dates have been derived for the paintings themselves (Newcomb 1967, pp. 40–41). It is the opinion of Gebhard (1960, pp. 32–33) that because of the apparent homogeneity of all the Pecos drawings, they were produced during a brief period of time, although no precise dates are suggested. In contrast, it is Newcomb's feeling that the tradition and the various periods therein represent a slow development and that

the earlier manifestations of the Pecos River Style may date several millennia before the birth of Christ (1967, p. 60). In Mile Canyon near Langtry, Texas Period 1 style paintings were found beneath midden refuse, a discovery which led to the conclusion that the paintings have considerable antiquity. Although the age of the rubble could not be determined, the cultural material contained therein appeared to be Archaic in nature (Newcomb 1967, p. 41). The terminal date for the Pecos River Style paintings is believed to be before the advent of the bow and arrow in the region, sometime between A.D. 600 and 1000, because of the lack of the representation of this weapon in the paintings.

The relevance of this to the Barrier Canyon Style is only general, owing to the possibly long period of time involved, as well as to a lack of understanding as to just how these two widely separated styles may be related. Nevertheless, it may be possible that considerable antiquity may be attributable to these works. Such conclusions support the hypothesis formulated earlier that the Barrier Canyon Style is not "Fremont' as now defined, although the similarities between the Fremont and the Barrier Canyon Styles are sufficient to suggest that the eastern Fremont rock art development was stimulated at least in part by a knowledge of these paintings. As the situation now exists, solid archaeological investigations will have to be made in order to prove or disprove these tentative conclusions.

VIII

The Relationships of The Fremont Culture to The Great Basin, The Southwest, and The Plains

One of the prime concerns in Fremont studies, from the earliest to the most recent treatises on the subject, has been the question of Fremont origins and contemporaneous cultural affiliations. The archaeology of Utah north and west of the San Juan was for many decades approached from the standpoint of its relation to the Basketmaker-Pueblo sequence and the designation of the area as the "Northern Periphery" tended to reinforce the concept of its culture as a diluted version of Southwestern developments. Nevertheless, even Morss, who pioneered the archaeology of the Fremont River region, thought that the Fremont culture was not an integral part of the main stream of Southwestern development and that it showed originality in many details, making it difficult to think of the Fremonters as merely a backward Southwestern tribe, even though he felt that "the influences which moulded the Fremont culture appear to have been Southwestern" (Morss 1931, pp. 77–78). As more work was done in the "Northern Periphery," it was increasingly believed that the cultural manifestations through much of the area resembled each other more than they did the Anasazi cultures to which they were regarded as peripheral, and the term "Northern Periphery" went out of favor.

The concept of an ancient, long-persisting, generalized, hunting and gathering Desert Culture was later advanced to provide the unifying element in Utah sites and the base out of which the Fremont configuration grew, partially in response to Anasazi influence, particularly in the Sevier Fremont region (Jennings and Norbeck 1955, Wormington 1955, Jennings and others 1956, Jennings 1957, Taylor 1957).

Recently the relationships between the Fremont culture and the Virgin Kayenta division of the Anasazi have been explored in some detail (Gun-nerson 1957, 1960, 1969; Anderson 1963; Ambler 1966a). Gunnerson proposes that the Fremont culture is the product of Puebloan people moving into the region from the Virgin area, any indigenous pre-Fremont culture or non-Puebloan culture outside the area making no substantial contribution to the Fremont development. Thus he thinks that the Desert Culture concept is not applicable as a Fremont base. Ambler also thinks that Pueblo traits from the Virgin Kayenta are manifest in the Fremont area, but supports the view that they arrived in the northern region by diffusion and not by an actual migration of peoples.

The possibility of a strong northern, ultimately Plains component in Fremont culture has been a matter of debate for some time. Wormington cites as evidence the presence of stone rings, calcite tempered pottery, moccasins, pictographs of shield-bearing anthropomorphs, and pyramidal dent corn of ultimately Mexican origin (1955, pp. 181–186). (The possibility that this type of corn came into the Fremont area from the northeast seems to be pretty well ruled out by later botanical studies. See Gunnerson 1969, Appendix I, Fremont Maize, by Galinat and Gunnerson; Cutler 1966b, pp. 15–19.) Taylor, however, although tracing the presence of horned headdresses, shields, and tear streaks in Fremont rock art to a Plains origin, is of the general opinion that Plains influence "is not appreciably noticeable, and only a very tenuous link can be implied on the basis of shield-like pictographs and rock enclosures," and regards Fremont moccasins and other leather goods as more likely to be of Basin origin (1957, pp. 128, 157–158). Gunnerson points to the absence of "the snub-nosed end scrapers and side scrapers which are so characteristic of Plains archaeological complexes of the past several thousand years" (1957, p. 30). More recently, however, a Plains origin hypothesis for the Fremont culture has been proposed by Sharrock (1966a) and Sharrock and Marwitt (1967), although at one point Sharrock (1966a, p. 164) suggests that its influence is limited to the northern portion of Fremont occupation.

In addition, Aikens developed the thesis in a series of publications (1966b, 1967a, 1967b) that the Fremont culture-bearers were Athabaskan immigrants from the Plains and that the culture itself resulted from a "coalescence of northern Plains and Southwestern Anasazi cultures" (1967a, p. ix). He further characterized the Anasazi influences as minor in the total Fremont development (1967b, p. 207), and dismissed the Desert Culture component emphasized by Jennings and Taylor with the statement that "perhaps cultural traditions of the Great Basin and Plateau will be found to have contributed, although such elements have not been identified at present" (1967a, p. ix).

On the basis of recent work in Hogup Cave in the region of Great Salt Lake, however, Aikens (1970) feels that a stronger continuity between the ancient Archaic or Desert Culture and the more recent Fremont culture should be recognized. It is also proposed by Aikens (1970) as well as others (Taylor 1970; Ambler 1970; Wormington, personal communication 1970) that the regional variations among the pre-Fremont cultures may very well account in part for the regionalism present in Fremont culture.

Some light on the controversial problem of the relationships of the Fremont culture may be shed by bringing to bear upon the subject the evidence available in the rock art. It should be stressed at the outset, however, that this art is no mere resultant of diverse external and internal influences but has developed in its own way as a distinctive manifestation. Ambler's ranking of the Fremont culture on a taxonomic level with Anasazi or Hohokam (1966a, p. 273) is strongly supported by the evidence of its rock art.

THE FREMONT AND THE GREAT BASIN

A resemblance between the Great Basin abstract designs and certain of those of the Fremont area has been suggested in the literature. Steward (1941, p. 334) mentions that in addition to the Fremont figures at the mouth of White Canyon there are Curvilinear petroglyphs like those of the Great Basin. In a later publication Hunt (1953, p. 179) also makes the observation that most of the abstract designs occurring in the La Sal Mountain region, an area in which both Fremont styles and Pueblo rock art styles are manifest, are "like those that occur in the Basin and Range province and to a lesser extent in the Plains." A review of the abstract elements listed in tables 1, 2, 3, and 5 of this paper as compared with those listed in Heizer and Baumhoff (1962, p. 173, table 3) for Nevada sites, suggests that a relatively significant percentage of abstract elements is shared between the Fremont area and the Great Basin. This data is summarized in table 8. (It was felt that the Great Basin Curvilinear Style sites in Nevada rather than those in Utah, tabulated in table 6, were a better item of comparison, as the Utah sites are subject to Fremont influences, see above, pp. 90–97.) Out of 37 abstract elements occurring in Nevada sites, 18, or 49 percent, appear in the panels of the Northern San Rafael zone, while 17, or 46 percent, are present in the Ashley-Dry Fork Uinta sites and in the Clear Creek Sevier A panels. The relatively small percentage of shared elements between the Dinosaur sites and the Great Basin may be due to the small number of sites recorded as well as to an actual reduction in variety of abstract figures in the Dinosaur district. Present in the Fremont rock art but absent in the Great Basin are enclosing wavy lines, enclosed decorated areas, rows of short lines, the scorpion motif, the maze, straight line, spiral with wavy lines, double spiral, the rectilinear spiral, and the compact geometric design. The latter four elements are distinctly Puebloan in character.

As described earlier in this paper, in Fremont sites the abstract elements are nearly always subsidiary to the representational motifs. As compared with the Great Basin sites, the circle complexes are simplified and the confusing entangling elements such as the involved curvilinear meanders have been dropped. It should also be pointed out that the one-pole ladder as it occurs in the Great Basin is frequently a much looser and more poorly defined element than its Fremont counterpart. This variation is consistent with the nature of the stylistic differences between the Great Basin sites and the Fremont.

The significance of the above discussion in light of a possible Fremont-Curvilinear Style relationship is not clear at the present time. It must be noted that elements such as the concentric circle, the spiral, and the wavy line which occur in the highest numbers in Fremont sites, as well as the wandering line, the zigzag, and rectilinear meander which occur in smaller percentages, are also shared with rock art panels of Anasazi origin (Steward 1941; Turner 1963, Schaafsma 1966b) and in a sense might be regarded as nearly universal motifs. Also of considerable significance is the fact that the remaining elements shared between the Fremont and the Great Basin occur in relatively small numbers in Fremont sites. At this juncture, then, a comparison of abstract elements occurring in Fremont rock art sites with those of the Great Basin suggests that the Great Basin Styles may have influenced the determination of abstract designs in Fremont work, but the evidence is not strong.

Regardless of the nature of the element correlation between the Great Basin rock art tradition and the Fremont styles discussed immediately above, other phenomena indicating a definite relationship between these two traditions in western Utah can be cited. To be taken into consideration here are stylistic characteristics which cannot be tabulated, for we are concerned not only with the element and its presence but also with the nuances of form. Thus, one finds in the western Utah sites an apparent modification of Fremont elements in a Great Basin Curvilinear Style direction such as was described earlier. It was also noted that the Curvilinear Style itself appears in turn to have been influenced by Fremont rock art. These phenomena indicate that the two traditions were indeed contemporaneous.

Consistent with this observation is the suggestion by Heizer and Baumhoff (1962, p. 233) that the Curvilinear Style is attributable to hunting and gathering groups occupying the area from 1000 B.C. to as late as 1500 A.D. Whether the observed influences of the Great Basin Curvilinear Style and the Fremont rock art on each other were due to simple diffusion between adjacent but differentiated cultural groups or, in fact, to a gradual adoption by hunting and gathering groups in western Utah of horticultural pottery and associated traits of Fremont culture, is a problem yet to be clarified.

PUEBLO–FREMONT RELATIONSHIPS

A number of elements and a certain stylistic emphasis in some Fremont rock art can be traced to Puebloan contact. This is especially true in the western Fremont regions where a direct connection between Fremont and Virgin Kayenta designs can be demonstrated. Of singular importance in this regard are features of many Fremont anthropomorphs that appear to have been adapted from the Cave Valley Style figures. The western Fremont anthropomorph with Cave Valley Style characteristics is relatively small in size compared to eastern Fremont anthropomorphic figures, and a triangular torso is preferred over a trapezoidal shape. A horizontal element at the apex of the body triangle, from which the legs may drop at right angles or which in the Fremont may be developed into a boat-shaped or rectangular device, appears in both Cave Valley Style and in western Fremont figures (figs. 85, 88, 89, 107, 109, 113, 122, 123, 126). Also shared is the practice of extending across the top of the head a line which may be terminated with downward pointing projections. Above the head of one Fremont anthropomorph from Upper Baker Creek Cave in Nevada is a line of dots which is further reminiscent of the Cave Valley Style development (fig. 109).

Elements shared by the western Fremont and the eastern Virgin Kayenta Style are the highly decorative rectilinear scrolls, or spirals, and the rectilinear meander (of a type described by Turner for Glen Canyon (1963, table 2), as opposed to the figure so named which is described in figure 21 of this paper) and the more complex abstract designs which resemble geometric pottery and textile decoration. The petroglyphs at Parowan Gap were found to exhibit dotted grids among other Virgin Kayenta pottery design motifs. Finally, but less specifically, herds of well-defined mountain sheep with rectangular bodies resemble Puebloan carvings in their decorative emphasis.

With the possible exception of occasional hand-holding anthropomorphs, a rare double spiral, and the spiral with wavy line, the last two elements being characteristic of Glen Canyon Style 4 (see "watchspring S scroll" and "line with single scroll," Turner 1963, table 2, pp. 3–4), specifically Anasazi elements in eastern Fremont sites have yet to be discovered. However, small solidly carved mountain sheep of the southern San Rafael manifest a decorative aesthetic quality suggestive of Fremont-Pueblo ties. Too general to be particularly significant in this regard are simple painted decorative panels in Nine Mile and Florence Canyons, although, again, the negative zigzag in Florence Canyon is a Style 4 motif (Turner 1963, table 2).

In this connection, the popularity of serpents, some plumed, in the northern San Rafael zone and the rare occurrence of flute players in the

Classic Vernal Style of the Uinta Fremont are of interest, particularly since they are scarce or lacking throughout the southern Fremont area. Possibly they reflect the Mesa Verde, rather than the San Juan Kayenta or Virgin Kayenta Anasazi contacts of the Fremont.

Worthy of consideration is the possibility that other traits shared by the eastern Fremont peoples and the late San Juan Kayenta groups were brought into the latter area through Fremont contact rather than the reverse. The presence in the Tsegi drainage, for example, of one-pole ladders and a preoccupation with sets of large concentric circles and other round motifs appearing in certain contexts as shields, raises the question of this possibility (Schaafsma 1966b, figs. 13, 20, 22, 35). The shield-bearing figure popularly known as "Bat Woman" at NA 2531 and the negative anthropomorphic figure in the large white circle at Betatakin (NA 2512) are particularly noteworthy in this regard (Schaafsma 1966b, figs. 21 and 15; Judd 1930, pl. 29 A). The latter is reminiscent of the negative Fremont anthropomorph inside a similar white shield device at Davis Gulch (pl. 16). The possibility of a Fremont to San Juan Kayenta trend is reinforced by other archaeological data. Investigations in southern Utah in the zone of Anasazi and Fremont contact revealed that there was little definable Puebloan influence on the Fremont in this region. Further evidence from the Coombs site near Boulder suggested that the flow of ideas and objects was rather from the Fremont to the Anasazi (Ambler 1966a, pp. 236–237). The presence of seemingly Fremont influence in Tsegi rock art might thus be explained by population movements in the northern Kayenta region. That the Kayenta people were in the process of expanding northward in late Pueblo II to mid Pueblo III into the southern periphery of Fremont occupation has been established. By A.D. 1200 and probably earlier, however, the abandonment of these Kayenta outposts began with a slow retreat southward and a concentrated occupation in the Tsegi, before this northern realm was completely deserted (Lister 1964, p. 81). Such population shifts could account for the popularity of the large circular designs in late Pueblo III Tsegi Phase sites dating between A.D. 1250 and 1300.

THE EASTERN FREMONT AND THE SAN JUAN BASKETMAKERS

As opposed to the Fremont anthropomorph in western Utah, which shares a number of features with the Virgin Kayenta Cave Valley Style figure, the representation of the human form in the eastern Fremont shows strong resemblances to the San Juan Basketmaker II anthropomorphic type. This relationship has been pointed out on numerous occasions (Morss 1931, p. 42; Steward 1936, p. 59, and 1937b, p. 421; Baldwin 1947, p. 35). Characteristics shared by the two are their dominant role, a trapezoidal as well as triangular body shape, and the presence in many cases of thin arms and legs and even splayed fingers. Although the head of some Basketmaker anthropomorphs may be abnormally small, in other instances the head is depicted as normal, as in the Fremont representations. The helmetlike headdress seen on certain Classic Vernal Style figures finds its prototype among Basketmaker figures in northeastern Arizona, as evidenced by the Painted Cave representations (Haury 1945, fig. 16 h). Other large trapezoidal anthropomorphs from the San Juan River near Bluff are depicted with tall headdresses of crescentlike elements unlike anything found in a Fremont context, but these same figures are also shown with simple necklaces and waist decoration reminiscent of Fremont detail (fig. 133 a). The hands and feet of the San Juan Basketmaker figures are shown in full, but in a drooping position. A similar treatment of these features may also occur in Fremont art, although in the latter, the feet are usually depicted to the side. Painted Basketmaker anthropomorphs from Grand Gulch also wear necklaces (fig. 133 b).

Of further interest here is a single additional Basketmaker figure from Buttress Canyon near Haury's Painted Cave. This figure, painted in solid green and nearly three feet high, holds in the left hand a triangular object which is highly similar to the stylized heads held by Fremont anthropomorphs (fig. 134).

The derivation of the eastern Fremont anthropomorph, particularly in the southern San Rafael zone, may be somewhat complicated by the influence of Barrier Canyon Style figures. Shared characteristics of the Fremont anthropomorphs and the Barrier Canyon Style figures were discussed earlier (p. 130). The common attributes in this case are generalized in nature and not as specific as between Basketmaker II and Fremont. It appears, however, that the Fremonters, the Barrier Canyon Style artists, and the San Juan Basketmakers were participants in a rock art tradition of the Colorado Plateau in which the human figure

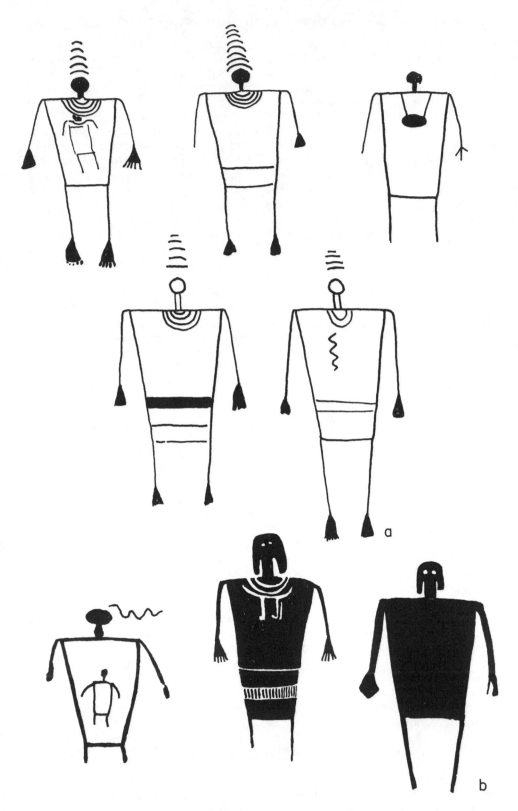

FIGURE 133 Basketmaker figures: a, petroglyphs, right bank of the San Juan River, one-half mile below Butler Wash. Figures are only partially reconstructed here due to the difficulty of seeing small details in the photograph. The figures are situated high on the cliff and suffer from erosion. Source: anonymous photo. b, Grand Gulch paintings. Source: A. V. Kidder photo.

FIGURE 134 Basketmaker figure from Buttress Canyon, Arizona.

was given unusual emphasis. This tradition may in turn have been related to a parallel religious configuration or ideology which provoked the numerous and heroic representations of the human form.

The significance of the Basketmaker-Fremont relationship in terms of the greater cultural configuration is not fully clear, and an apparent time gap between the two cultures has yet to be reconciled. The Basketmaker II culture dates roughly between the first and fifth centuries A.D., although a Basketmaker II tree-ring date of A.D. 700 in the Navajo Mountain area suggests that this cultural manifestation may have persisted later in fringe regions (Ambler 1969, p. 111). Nevertheless, we are still left with a 250- to 300-year gap between this date and the earliest dates for the Fremont

culture estimated by Ambler (1970), Breternitz (1970), and Gunnerson (1969). A remaining problem is the difficulty of knowing just how late Basketmaker type art persisted. The association of large anthropomorphic paintings and Basketmaker II habitation sites in northern Arizona has been reasonably well established by early investigators (Kidder and Guernsey 1919, p. 198). Roberts (1929, p. 122) claims to have found these figures in southeastern Utah as petroglyphs associated with Basketmaker III sites. The resemblances between the Basketmaker rock paintings and carvings and the later Fremont developments, nevertheless, are strongly indicative of Fremont connections with the earlier phases of cultural development in the San Juan region.

THE FREMONT AND THE NORTHERN PLAINS

The problem of the presence of Plains influence in Fremont rock art is a difficult one for a number of reasons. The significance of the shared characteristics that do exist between the Plains art and that of the Fremont is often obscured by the lack of well-dated Plains sites. Furthermore, as yet, documentation of northern Plains rock art sites is spotty, and a clear picture has yet to be constructed. More specifically, the nature of the rock art on the northern Plains before the advent of the Fremont culture around A.D. 950 or 1000 has yet to be defined.

Difficulties like these make the elements such as the shield motif, the horned headdresses, and the weeping eye, which are commonly cited as evidence to illustrate northern Plains influence on the Fremont culture, hard to assess. Among these elements, the shield motif has received the most attention and discussion regarding its point of origin and path of diffusion. Wormington (1955, p. 186) and Aikens (1967b, p. 201) subscribe to the idea that the shield as it appears in northern Plains sites is antecedent to its appearance in the Fremont. In support of this argument, Wormington states that the similarities between the Montana and Wyoming shield-bearing anthropomorphs and those of the Fremont are too striking to be coincidental, and believes that the wide distribution of the shield on the northern Plains indicates that this is basically a northern trait. On the other hand, in a recent comprehensive study of the shield element as it appears in Plains rock art by Gebhard (1966), it was concluded that, if one assumes that the shield motif is a basic element of the classic Fremont culture, and accepts as correct a terminal date of A.D. 1150 as postulated by Wormington, then the shield motif in the Fremont apparently antedates the occurrence of this motif in the Plains to the north and east and in the rock art to the west in Nevada and California. In sum, Gebhard thinks that the evidence suggests that the shield figure ultimately has a Mexican origin in North America and makes its first northern appearance among the Pecos River Style paintings of the Rio Grande. From here, its next earliest known depiction seems to be in the rock art of the Fremont culture, from which it subsequently spread into the Plains area, where it appeared in the latter part of the late prehistoric period from about A.D. 1000 to 1500 and continued to be used in the protohistoric period and into historic times (1966, p. 730). Unfortunately, Gebhard does not really explain his reasons for estimating the appearance of the shield figure between A.D. 1000

to 1500 in the late Prehistoric Horizon in northern Plains sites. According to Mulloy (1970, personal communication), although the rock art of Pictograph Cave near Billings, Montana, including the shield figures, correlates with this horizon, the horizon dates from A.D. 500 to 1500, and there is no possibility of relating the rock art to any specific subperiod within this time span. Thus, unless this can be accomplished, the occurrence of these figures in Pictograph Cave offers no clues to the problem at hand at the current time.

At one point, Gebhard (1966, p. 730) questions whether or not the shields in association with Fremont rock drawings might be later intrusions. He points out that the shield bearers differ considerably from the Basketmaker-inspired trapezoidal figures typical of Fremont representations and that shields are lacking in Basketmaker art. I am of the opinion, however, that, although the shield bearer is in certain respects typologically at variance with the more traditional human form, it is, nevertheless, stylistically consistent with the latter in all its regional variations, and that this factor indicates that the shield figure is a well-integrated trait of the Fremont rock art development. Furthermore, Fremont anthropomorphs from the Vernal-Dinosaur district in the Uinta region, from Glen Canyon in the southern San Rafael zone, and in the Conger region are shown with small shields in hand.

Gebhard's hypothetical reconstruction of the diffusion of the shield motif is of further interest in this study in regard to the affinities discovered between the Barrier Canyon Style and the Pecos River paintings and the appearance of a shield in one Barrier Canyon Style painting at the Head of Sinbad (photograph, Bureau of Land Management Office, Price, Utah). As pointed out earlier, the nature of the relationship between the Barrier Canyon Style anthropomorphs at Moab and the shields is ambiguous. This entire relationship bears further investigation.

Other subscribers to the hypothesis that the Fremont shield motif moved out of the Fremont of Utah onto the Plains are Grant (1967) and Buckles (1964). The latter postulates that the shield figure moved out of Utah around A.D. 1150 into western Wyoming and Montana prior to the Historic Period beginning around A.D. 1800. From here, he contends, the trait spread in the Historic Period to areas further north, east, and south on the Plains (Buckles 1964, p. 182). This rather simple scheme is somewhat complicated, however, by the observation that the shield motif occurring in the Pottery Mound Pueblo IV kiva paintings and in the Pueblo IV petroglyphs on the Rio Grande are believed to date as early as the 15th century (Schaafsma 1968, p. 21, and Grant 1967, p. 65). Furthermore, other shield figures have been noted in Jornada Branch Mogollon rock art which date no later than about 1400 (Newcomb 1967, pl. 128, and Gebhard 1966, p. 729). The shield motif in both instances may have been ultimately derived from early southern Plains contacts. For further discussion of the diffusion of the shield motif, see Gebhard 1966 and Grant 1967, pp. 61–65).

In conclusion, the problem of the earliest appearance of the shield motif in the rock art of the Fremont is still open to speculation in the absence of sound dating for its prehistoric occurrences in the northern Plains. As the situation now stands, however, there is nothing to indicate an earlier Plains occurrence, and a Fremont source for the diffusion of this motif to the northern Plains seems more likely. The shared shield motif thus affords no positive support to the theory that the Fremont culture had in part a northern Plains origin.

The weeping-eye motif and the occurrence of horned headdresses are even less well documented. Nevertheless, a definite connection of some sort between these elements in Plains and in Fremont rock art seems to be indicated, as with the shield, by the fact that the weeping eye and horned headdress are traits well developed in both of these areas and are rare or absent in contemporary or earlier rock art of Puebloan or Great Basin origin. Both devices occur on the shield bearers of the Late Prehistoric horizon in Pictograph Cave (Wormington 1955, figs. 60 and 61). Horned headdresses are also present on over half the figures from the Dinwoody site in western Wyoming (Gebhard and Cahn 1950, p. 226). As the result of a recent study of the weeping-eye motif, Buckles concludes that this device falls into two major types: the diagonal line type occurring in the western periphery of the Plains and the zigzag type occurring in the eastern Plains (1964, p. 143). For the zigzag line type, which often appears in Southern Cult-like contexts, he suggests an Eastern Woodland origin. The diagonal line type is used exclusively in the Fremont, and although Buckles suggests that a Fremont origin for this type is possible (1964, p. 139), a quantity of dated material is necessary before the nature of Plains-Fremont connections can be postulated on the basis of this shared motif.

Of distinctly minor significance in terms of the

total Fremont rock art configuration, but possibly of some import in actually demonstrating northern impact on Fremont designs, are the owl figures present in two Fremont sites and certain stylistic aberrations evident in a very small number of Uinta Fremont panels. An owllike personage with fringed wings appears in one Vernal site (fig. 17), and on Diamond Creek in the southern Uinta region (Wormington 1955, fig. 50). The distribution of this rare figure in the more northern and eastern portions of the eastern Fremont area, and the occurrence of a number of winged owllike personages in the Dinwoody, Wyoming sites (Grant 1967, p. 133, and Gebhard and Cahn 1950, p. 226), suggest that this feature actually may have been transmitted to the Fremont area from Wyoming, but again careful dating is necessary.

Stylistic features bearing northern likenesses in Fremont territory show a similar but more confined distribution. In one Vernal site and in two Brush Creek panels anthropomorphs carelessly rendered are short and squat in general aspect (figs. 135 and 136). These figures lack the grace and nicety of proportion characteristic of most Uinta Fremont anthropomorphs and their decorative elements tend to be jumbled and crowded. Heads of certain figures are absent. At another Fremont site near Vernal, there is an anthropomorph with atrophied arms, an unusual feature among Vernal representations. These deviant Uinta figures to some degree resemble anthropomorphs from the Flaming Gorge area in extreme northern Utah and Wyoming (Day and Dibble 1963) and anthropomorphic figures from the vicinity of Dinwoody, Wyoming, (Gebhard and Cahn 1950). Although the Flaming Gorge figures have undergone certain fundamental stylistic changes, the presence of trapezoidal-bodied and horned anthropomorphs, necklaces, and shield bearers in this region suggests that actual Fremont occupation occurred here. This possibility is substantiated by the presence of Turner Gray sherds from one Flaming Gorge site (Day and Dibble 1963, p. 39).

The Dinwoody anthropomorphs manifest their own peculiarities, among which they share with the aberrant northern Fremont petroglyphs a squat configuration, circular and crowded body decoration, and rudimentary arms with large splayed fingers. At this juncture a comparison between the Dinwoody petroglyphs and the Fremont figures is not intended necessarily to indicate a direct or specific relationship between them, but rather to illustrate general tendencies present in some of the rock art north of the Fremont area in Wyoming. The Dinwoody figures of this style have not been dated except on a relative basis and documentation is lacking in the area between Dinwoody and northern Fremont sites. Finally, as these stylistic trends are apparent in only four out of well over a hundred Uinta panels, the significance of the shared traits that do exist is small.

Plains styles may have been operative in modifying the Fremont rock art on its eastern edge, as manifested in the Diamond Creek and Westwater Draw sites, although, as usual, there are not sufficient dates and rock art studies in the Plains regions to the north and east to allow sound comparisons along these lines at the current time. The absence of the trapezoidal anthropomorph in this locality is notable, and the only familiar Fremont figure depicted here is the shield bearer (Wormington 1955, figs. 49 and 51). The long, curved spears and other devices projecting from the edges of shields and the radiating lines and the relatively long legs of the anthropomorphs combine to give these figures a lighter and more mobile quality than is found in more typical Fremont representations to the west. As these latter characteristics are qualities shared with certain Plains styles, a connection might be suggested.

In spite of the length of the foregoing discussion, one can only conclude that the currently demonstrable northern Plains influence in Fremont rock art is fairly insignificant and present, at most, only on the northern and northeastern edges of Fremont occupation. On the other hand, northern Plains traits appear to be more prevalent in the broader archaeological picture, as evidenced by Fremont skeletal material and by linguistic reconstruction (Sharrock and Marwitt 1967, p. 1), and by architectural design, bone tool types, and possibly other features enumerated by Aikens (1967b, pp. 201–202).

The shield and weeping-eye motifs and horned headdresses appearing in the rock art throughout the entire length of the eastern Fremont area and extending here and there into the western area are somewhat problematical. As described above, these three features also occur in Plains sites and are essentially lacking in contemporaneous or earlier Puebloan and Great Basin sites, thus indicating a definite connection of some nature between the northern Plains and Fremont in this regard. That these features appeared earlier in the northern Plains than in the Fremont, however, has not been demonstrated. It is even possible that these motifs appeared first in the Fremont sites from whence they eventually spread into the northern Plains area. This hypothesis was advanced earlier by Buckles (1964, pp. 181–182) in regard to the shield motif, and the hypothesis is consonant with the archaeological possibility that at the time the Fremont region was abandoned, the Fremont people dispersed northward through the Wyoming-Plains corridor due to the pressure of Shoshonean expansion (Sharrock 1966a, p. 169; and Sharrock and Marwitt 1967, p. 1). Finally, it is also possible that the features under consideration were manifested nearly contemporaneously in the Fremont and Plains rock art as a result of stimulation from a third source.

FIGURE 135 Anthropomorphs from Brush Creek of the Vernal-Dinosaur District showing apparent northern stylistic influences. Source: Reagan-Nusbaum photo, BP 6.

FIGURE 136 Anthropomorphs from Brush Creek in the Vernal Dinosaur District showing apparent northern stylistic influences. Source: Reagan-Nusbaum photo, BP 3.

CONCLUSIONS

From the foregoing discussion it is apparent that certain major contributing outside influences evident in Fremont rock art are traceable to the Pueblo and Basketmaker culture of the Southwest. In western Utah, particularly in that region of central western Utah just north of the Virgin Kayenta area, it was found that the inventory of abstract elements in the rock paintings and carvings received a notable increment of traits selected from the Puebloan repertoire of the Virgin Kayenta immediately to the south. In addition, the Fremont anthropomorphic figure, so characteristic of the Fremont rock art, takes on, in the western area, attributes of the Cave Valley Style anthropomorph, as opposed to the Basketmaker-inspired figure dominant in the eastern Fremont regions. To the north and east, specific Puebloan influences appear to dwindle quickly, and those that do occur may more likely be derived from the San Juan Anasazi region than the Virgin Kayenta. In conclusion, the presence of a relatively strong Virgin Kayenta influence on the rock art of the western Fremont area is consistent with the greater archae-

ological picture; i.e., that (1) the Virgin Kayenta best fits the archaeological evidence as the place of origin of most Puebloan traits found in the Fremont, and (2) the Fremont of west central Utah received the largest number of these traits (Ambler 1966a, pp. 255 and 267; Anderson 1963; and Gunnerson 1960). It should be noted that the Puebloan influences cited above by no means suggest a wholesale importation of Anasazi traits into the Fremont area, but reflect instead a process of selective borrowing. Thus, there is no particular evidence in the rock art for a Puebloan migration such as was postulated by Gunnerson (1969), and the concept of trait diffusion suggested by Ambler (1966a) seems more feasible.

In the eastern Fremont area, the large trapezoidal figure finds its prototype in the Basketmaker anthropomorph, although certain simplified anthropomorphs in the Southern San Rafael zone manifest traits in common with figures in the Barrier Canyon Style, a possible archaic or proto-Fremont predecessor in this region. The specialized development of the anthropomorphic figure

throughout the entire Fremont area and particularly in the eastern half, and in addition, the
selection and emphasis of certain abstract designs,
particularly the large spiral and concentric circle,
are responsible in a major way for the emergence
of Fremont rock art into a distinctive configuration
of its own. Other characteristically Fremont motifs, such as the shield and shield bearer, the
weeping eye, and the horned headdress, may be
local Fremont developments or additions from an
as yet undefinable outside source to the north or
east which were developed into major themes by
the Fremonters. Northern Plains stylistic influences, detectable in a very few Uinta sites, were
never a contributing factor as such to the Fremont
development and never penetrated into the greater Fremont area.

Finally, it is possible that the rock art of certain
preagricultural groups in western Utah had some
bearing on the subsequent Fremont rock art developments in that area. In the Great Basin of
western Utah, a certain amount of integration
of Fremont motifs and the Great Basin Curvilinear
Style occurs. However, as pointed out earlier,
whether this phenomenon indicates a direct continuity between the Desert cultures of the area
and the Fremont, or subsequent diffusion from
one cultural group to the other after the Fremont
culture was established is not clear.

IX

Interpretation

Inevitably, a study such as this raises questions concerning the meaning of the various groups of rock art that have been considered and the purposes for which they were made. Unfortunately, these are among the most difficult of considerations, especially in this case, when the study has been made largely from photographs which, as already pointed out, lack data on the associated material, site situations, and other related factors that might be pertinent to the investigation of the function of these panels. Thus, in considering these questions, one is limited to a few chance observations made by previous investigators and to clues extracted from the rock representations themselves.

THE VIRGIN KAYENTA

Very little is known about the purpose or significance of the Virgin Kayenta petroglyphs. The design elements are often abstract, and, with the exception of the Cave Valley Style, the human figure receives no special emphasis. The presence and popularity of mountain sheep, deer, and other animal representations in these panels reflects an interest in the game animals, and some sort of magical relationship might be implied between the representation and the creature itself. The pattern of occurrence of the bulk of Puebloan rock art, however, at least among the Kayenta, does not appear similar to patterns of occurrence observed for petroglyphs used in hunting magic in the Great Basin (Heizer and Baumhoff 1962). In the Tsegi (Schaafsma 1966b) and in the Glen Canyon of the Kayenta area, the majority of rock paintings and carvings occur in or near habitation sites, although Turner also mentions their presence near springs, along trails, and at fords, crossings, and other sites of human activity in the latter region (1963, p. 28). Similarly, the Virgin Kayenta sites frequently occur in association with habitation sites or shelters (Wauer 1965; Steward, 1941). At Atlatl Rock, however, in the western Virgin Kayenta area of Nevada, Puebloan motifs occur with Great Basin Abstract petroglyphs on a group of isolated boulders (Heizer and Baumhoff 1962, p. 28). The site might have been a watering place for game, since on the south edge of one of the rocks there is a dammed natural basin large enough to hold about 1000 gallons of water. Providing the dam is aboriginal in origin, these authors suggest that the spot may have been used by Indians as a point of ambush for mountain sheep or antelope, and that the petroglyphs may have been associated with this practice. In sum, the motivations for the creation of the designs are complex, and their making is not attributable to a single purpose.

THE FREMONT

At present, the significance and purpose of the Fremont rock art are also unclear. The fact that this art appears to be coeval with the advent of horticulture in Utah does not seem to signify that it was directly related to horticultural practices. The intermingling of Fremont type figures with the Curvilinear Style in western Utah suggests that at least on occasion these figures may have been made for similar reasons.

According to Heizer and Baumhoff (1962, pp. 6–15 and 210–225), the Great Basin Abstract petroglyphs appear to have been done as a part of magic hunting ritual and were thus related to subsistence practices of this order. In a combined study of petroglyph locations and game trails, they found that the bulk of Nevada petroglyphs were located apart from habitation sites in spots suitable for game taking, and that they were absent from locations unfit for this activity (1962, p. 241). They further postulate that many of the petroglyph sites were used in communal hunts in which a shaman would perform the necessary magical rites, including the making of petroglyphs. Many of these sites show evidence of use over a considerable period of time.

It would be of interest in western Utah to see if a distributional and hence functional difference might occur between Sevier Style A sites showing a strong Anasazi influence and those displaying the proposed Sevier Style B work (see pp. 91–92).

Ambler (1970) has observed that in many instances in western Utah and eastern Nevada Fremont remains seem to be results of periodic hunting forays by Fremont people into areas not occupied permanently, as these remains often occur in areas in which horticulture was not feasible. Such a suggestion would account in part for the Fremont rock art occurring in the western fringe of Fremont activity. Furthermore, in contradistinction to Sharrock (see page 51 above), Ambler (1970) suggests that the presence of Fremont rock art south and east of the Colorado River where there is little evidence of Fremont occupation, is an indication that this region was used as a hunting ground by Fremont people, either predating the Mesa Verde occupation there or contemporary with it.

Breternitz has observed in Dinosaur National Monument that rock art sites "are generally not found at Fremont dwelling sites nor do the rock art panels usually show definite evidence of having served also as habitation locations by Fremont peoples" (1970, p. 6). He does not, however, further describe site situations or suggest what their function may have been.

It should be noted that Fremont rock art does not always occur apart from Fremont habitation sites. In the Stein Shelter in Meadow Valley in eastern Nevada, Fowler (1970) reports finding Fremont type figures and a Fremont occupational level. In eastern Utah south of the Uinta region, rock shelters containing other cultural remains frequently are decorated with paintings or petroglyphs (Gunnerson 1957).

Finally, as was noted earlier, the black boulder petroglyphs in the San Rafael seem to occur regularly near open rock circle sites and are always on a hillside facing downward and away from the houses (Morss 1931, p. 34). Considering both the situation and attitude of the latter, a magical protective function might be hypothesized.

Regardless of their situation, the high degree of development of petroglyphs and rock paintings

and the widespread distribution of the horned and usually dominant anthropomorphic figures suggest that Fremont rock art not only held an important place in Fremont culture but was one manifestation of a religious development which, with regional variations, was shared throughout the Fremont area. Emphasis on the anthropomorphic figure may reflect ideas of proto-Fremont or Basketmaker origin that were developed further by the Fremonters. The ceremonial nature of the attire of many of the figures, including masks, elaborate headdresses, and painted or tattooed facial and body decoration, as well as kilts, belts, pendants, and necklaces, strongly suggests that they served some ritual function. The parallels between these figures and those in the clay figurine tradition, which is believed to have functioned in a religious context, support this view (Morss 1954, p. 62, and Taylor 1957, p. 45). It is impossible to know if the human figures depicted in these panels are supernaturals or human beings in ceremonial gear, or if, indeed, this distinction is even important. That many of these figures wear horns may signify that they are bearers of special power, as horned figures in Southwestern iconography have this attribute. Hunting activities and warfare are two themes recurrent in the content. Bison, elk, deer, and mountain sheep are depicted, occasionally in hunting scenes, and the importance of hunting in the Fremont economy is well established by the archaeological remains. Concern with warfare can be inferred from the ceremonially attired figures of the eastern area which hold shields in their hands or wear large shields covering their entire body. In the Uinta region the Fremont anthropomorph may be depicted carrying what appears to be a trophy head and a few anthropomorphic figures are shown surrounded by arrows. One Classic Vernal figure has an arrowhead depicted on his chest. A word of caution might be justified, however, in this interpretation, as the apparel of war could also signify symbolic or ceremonial conflicts relating to natural forces and not necessarily human strife (Schaafsma 1968, p. 23). Nevertheless, Wormington, in reporting her excavations at the Turner-Look site, describes an unusually large number of arrow points which she thinks indicate a greater emphasis on either hunting or warfare than is evident in the Southwest (1955, p. 86). In addition, she found at this site what she thinks may be evidence of cannibalism and a trophy mandible (1955, p. 87).

It would appear, in any case, that the themes depicted in the Fremont rock art are activities which were primarily the concern of the Fremont men. Undoubtedly the women were involved in gathering activities and presumably in horticultural practices, especially in a culture in which hunting, a male activity, was of major importance. Thus, the rock art in which hunting and possibly warfare, whether real or ceremonial in nature, are represented would seem to be the production of the male population. It might be further proposed that a culture which had obtained a certain measure of security through the raising and storing of cultivated crops possibly allowed the male population greater opportunity to develop elaborate art and ritual around the practices of hunting and warfare. By the same token, the Fremont population with its growing and stored crops was probably more susceptible to attack from wandering bands. Not only would the food supply of such a group be highly coveted by outsiders, but the sedentary or semisedentary nature of the gardeners would make them more vulnerable to hit-and-run attackers, and a cult of warfare might be stimulated to develop (Carter 1945, p. 75). A study of the location of habitation sites would contribute to an understanding of whether or not the Fremont population appeared to be threatened in this way.

THE BARRIER CANYON STYLE

Of the rock art considered in this study, the Barrier Canyon Style is perhaps the most tantalizing and, at the same time, the most elusive in its significance. As Gunnerson (1969, p. 63) has observed, the remoteness of many of these panels from significant habitation sites suggests that they were painted in isolated ceremonial centers or retreats. It is also notable that each panel is for the most part consistent in its technique of execution and in its individual stylistic peculiarities, suggesting that each was painted by only one person and does not represent the work of a group of different individuals. Such a person may have been chosen for this purpose alone or may have functioned in some ritual office which involved the creation of these paintings.

As with the Fremont material or the Pecos River paintings, (Newcomb 1967) a key to the meaning and purpose in the Barrier Canyon Style art lies in the anthropomorphic beings. The concept of supernatural powers attributable to anthropomorphic form does seem to be implicit. Of course, one cannot be certain whether supernatural beings or men in ceremonial attire are portrayed, but in this case, the former seems more likely. The ghostly death image, specific to this style, cannot be ignored. Upon viewing these paintings, one cannot help speculating that they were part of some sort of ancestor worship ritual which in turn served not one, but a variety of functions concerning the relationship of the Indians to their environment. The Indian's concern with his natural surroundings comes through profoundly in this art. There is no indication that they had to do with the hunt specifically, as hunt scenes are lacking in the documented material. If the seedbeater, sickle, and burden baskets portrayed in connection with wild plants are correctly interpreted, then it is possible that the paintings were in part related to the ritual surrounding food-gathering practices.

**Table 1.   Elements and Attributes of 98 Sites of the Classic Vernal Style in Ashley —
Dry Fork Valleys near Vernal, Utah**

A.   Major Element Categories

		Occurrences No.	%	Sites No.
Large Anthropomorph:	outline	239		72
(see B below)	no outline	81		24
	solid	33		16
	Total	353	44	83
Small anthropomorph:	outline	6		6
	stick or solid	71		19
	Total	77	10	22
Fluteplayer		5	t	4
Total all anthropomorphs		435	54	90
Quadruped:	outline	25		8
	solid	126		22
	Total (including 38 mountain sheep and 9 deer)	151	19	26
Other representational elements:	serpent	6		3
	bear paw print	5		1
	hand- or footprint	15		5
	shield (alone)	2		2
	Total	28	3	8
All representational elements		614	76	90
Abstract elements (see C below)		190	24	42
Total all elements		804	100	98*

* Obviously more than one element is often present at a site.

B.   Attributes of Large Anthropomorphs

		Occurrences No.	%	Sites No.
Headgear:	rake horns	5	1	4
	helmet	28	8	9
	inverted bucket	5	1	5
	inverted bucket and plumes	7	2	3
	horned	44	13	23
	other	98	28	40
	none visible	166	47	43
	Total	353	100	83

The author's original material from which Tables 1–8 have been prepared is in the Peabody Museum Archives.

Table 1. (Continued)

B.   Attributes of Large Anthropomorphs (continued)

		Occurrences		Sites
		No.	% *	No.
Torso:	trapezoidal	172	49	50
	naturalistic	12	3	5
	shield	25	7	13
Facial features		231	65	64
Tear streaks		19	5	13
Earbobs		38	11	21
Bead necklace		84	24	37
Yoke necklace		60	17	30
Arm bands		11	3	9
Vertical torso line		31	9	16
Dot body decoration		19	5	8
Patterned body decoration		8	2	4
Kilt		35	10	15
Holds:	shield	3	1	3
	head	19	5	12
	rake	2	t	2
In arcs or hoops		6	2	5
With arrows		11	3	3

* Based on a total of 353, see opposite page.

C.   Abstract Elements

	Occurrences		Sites
	No.	%	No.
Wavy line	17	9	9
Concentric circle	42	22	16
Dots or dot design	5	3	4
Spiral	27	14	15
Circle	11	6	7
Wandering line	9	5	7
Rectilinear meander	3	2	2
One-pole ladder	15	8	4
Circle or form cluster	3	2	3
Enclosing wavy line	4	2	4
Rake	14	7	5
Sawtooth	1	t	1
Zigzag	1	t	1
Enclosed decorated area	4	2	4
Row of short lines	3	2	3
Asterisk	1	t	1
Sun disc	7	4	4
Spoked or segmented circle	2	1	2
Circle with dot	4	2	4
Scorpion	1	t	1
Plant form	5	3	4
Maze	5	3	3
Straight line	3	2	3
Double spiral	2	1	1
Cross	1	t	1
Total	190	100	42

All of the sites recorded in Table 1 are petroglyphs sites, although it is possible that painting may have occurred originally in conjunction with the carving technique in certain instances. The distinction between "large" and "small" anthropomorphs may be questionable in certain cases, although it is generally valid on a typological basis in both the Vernal and the Dinosaur sites. Note that "fluteplayer" is a separate category from both "large" and "small" anthropomorphs in both Table 1 and Table 2. "t" equals trace.

**Table 2.   Elements and Attributes at 15 Sites of the Classic
Vernal Style in Dinosaur National Monument**

A.   Major Element Categories

| | | Occurrences | | Sites |
		No.	%	No.
Large anthropomorph:	outline	25		6
	no outline	13		4
	solid	23		6
	dot (drilled?)	15		3
	other	10		
	Total	86	37	11
Small anthropomorph:	outline	2		2
	solid or stick	24		4
	other	2		2
	Total	28	12	7
Fluteplayer		2	1	2
All anthropomorphs		116	50	7
Quadruped:	outline	5		2
	solid	61		9
	Total	66	28	10
Other representational:	animal tracks	7		2
	hand- or footprint	13		4
	Total	20	8	4
All representational elements		202	86	15
Abstract elements		32	14	8
Total all elements		234	100	15

B.   Attributes of Large Anthropomorphs

| | | Occurrences | | Sites |
		No.	%	No.
Headgear:	rake horns	2	2	2
	helmet	1	1	1
	inverted bucket	4	5	3
	Inverted bucket with plumes	3	4	3
	horned	12	14	3
	other	20	23	3
	none visible	44	51	10
	Total	86	100	11

Table 2. (continued)

B. Attributes of Large Anthropomorphs (continued)

		Occurrences		Sites
		No.	%	No.
Torso:	trapezoidal	19	22	5
	shield	1	1	1
Facial features		46	54	8
Tear streaks		1	1	1
Earbobs		15	18	4
Bead necklace		23	27	4
Yoke necklace		19	22	4
Vertical torso line		7	8	3
Dot body decoration		6	7	2
Kilt		6	7	3
Holds:	shield	5	6	2
	head	5	6	1
In arcs or hoops		1	1	1
With arrows		1	1	1

C. Kinds of Quadruped

	Occurrences		Sites
	No.	%	No.
Mountain sheep	40	61	8
Deer	6	9	3
Bison	5	8	2
Lizard	8	12	3
Unidentified	7	10	6
Total	66	100	10

D. Abstract Elements

	Occurrences		Sites
	No.	%	No.
Wavy line	7	22	4
Concentric circle	6	19	3
Dots or dot design	1	3	1
Spiral	10	32	3
Circle	3	9	1
One-pole ladder	1	3	1
Spiral with wavy line	1	3	1
Row of short lines	1	3	1
Sun disc	2	6	2
Total	32	100	

Thirteen of the panels in Table 2 are carved and two painted. One site (42Un37) contains horses and modern inscriptions in addition to the elements plotted here.

Table 3. Elements and Attributes at 85 Sites of the Northern San Rafael Style

A. Major Element Categories

| | | Occurrences | | Sites |
		No.	%	No.
Anthropomorph:	outline	28		14
	solid or stick	212		62
	other	11		4
	Total	251	20	68
Quadruped:	outline	33		11
	solid	349		52
	other	34		6
	Total	416	34	61
Other representational:	bird	31		7
	serpent	21		12
	shield	8		2
	animal tracks	7		6
	hand- or footprint	22		6
	Total	89	7	31
All representational elements		756	61	83
Abstract elements		479	39	65
Total all elements		1235	100	85

B. Attributes of Anthropomorphs

| | | Occurrences | | Sites |
		No.	%	No.
Headgear:	rake horns	9	35	7
	horned	65	8	29
Torso:	trapezoidal	88	3	33
	triangular	19	4	7
	shield	7	26	6
Holds staff or spear		4	2	3
Hunting		13	5	10

C. Kinds of Quadruped

| | Occurrences | | Sites |
	No.	%	No.
Mountain sheep	179	43	44
Deer and elk	119	28	11
Bison	12	3	11
Unidentified cloven-hoofed	15	4	10
Other unidentified	91	22	45
Total	416	100	61

Table 3. (continued)

D. Abstract Elements

	Occurrences		Sites
	No.	%	No.
Wavy lines	80	17	37
Concentric circles	25	5	15
Dots or dot design	54	11	20
Spiral	15	3	13
Circle	30	6	12
Wandering line	24	5	14
Circle or form cluster	8	2	6
One-pole ladder	5	1	5
Enclosing wavy lines	4	1	4
Connected circles	5	1	3
Rake	3	1	3
Sawtooth	17	4	7
Zigzag	12	3	7
Spiral with wavy line	1	t	1
Enclosed decorated area	5	1	4
Row of short lines	21	4	3
Asterisk or cross	7	1	6
Sun disc	1	t	1
Spoked circle	3	1	3
Circle with dot	10	2	7
Lozenge chain	3	1	3
Scorpion	1	t	1
Straight line	8	2	6
Double spiral	1	t	1
Circle chain	1	t	1
Decorated painted panel	4	1	2
Other or unidentified	131	27	34
Total	479	100	65

Sixty-nine of the panels in Table 3 are carved, 11 are painted and at 5 there are both paintings and carvings. The sites plotted are in Nine Mile Canyon, Jack Canyon, Range Creek, Green River, Florence Canyon, Chandler Canyon, Willow Creek, and Hill Creek. One site, ET–6–7 on Willow Creek, displays a number of freshly carved figures, including horseback riders, in addition to the tabulated elements.

Table 4.   Elements and Attributes at 16 Sites of Barrier Canyon Style

A.   Major Element Categories

		Occurrences		Sites
		No.	%	No.
Anthropomorph:	elongate, tapered	210		16
	elongate, rectangular	20		5
	broad, trapezoidal	3		1
	broad, triangular	5		2
	Total	238	79	16
Quadruped:	big dog	6		5
	mountain sheep	11		2
	pouch-type	3		3
	other	15		15
	Total (including 11 in composition and 13 flanking anthropomorphs)	35	12	9
Other representational:	bird (all flanking anthropomorphs)	22		3
	wild plant (not including plants held by anthropomorphs)	2		2
	other	5		4
	Total	29	9	7
All representational elements		302	100	
Abstract elements		1	t	1
Total all elements		303	100	10

Table 4. (continued)

B. Attributes of Anthropomorphs

| | | Occurrences | | Sites |
		No.	%	No.
Headgear:	series of short lines	5	2	4
	antennae	15	6	6
	rabbit ears	7	3	4
	horns	9	4	5
	dot crown	8	3	3
	other	19	8	7
	none visible	175	74	14
	Total	238	100	16
Torso decoration:	textile	8	3	2
	dots	17	7	4
	stripes	9	4	6
	dots and stripes	1	t	1
	inset panel	8	3	4
	other	26	11	5
	plain	169	72	15
	Total	238	100	16
Arms:	present	41	17	9
	lacking	197	83	16
	Total	238	100	16
Held in hand:	wild plant	4		3
	shield (?)	2		1
	snake	1		1
	other	7		2
	Total	14	6	5
Eyes		8	3	3
Earrings		6	2	5
Arcs		2	t	1
Flanked by wavy lines		12	5	5
Flanked by other design		6	2	4

Table 4 was made from photographs before a field trip to the sites. There are, therefore, some discrepancies between the table and the text, the latter taking into account certain field observations.

Table 5.   Elements and Attributes of 29 Sites of Sevier Style A in Clear Creek Canyon

A.   Major Element Categories

| | | Occurrences | | Sites |
		No.	%	No.
Anthropomorph:	outline	3		3
	solid	28		17
	stick	12		5
	Total	43	11	19
Quadruped:	solid	106		19
	stick	6		3
	Total	112	28	19
Bird		15	4	6
Tracks		1	t	1
Hand- or footprint		20	5	4
All representational elements		191	48	25
Abstract elements		211	52	23
Total all elements		402	100	29

B.   Attributes of Anthropomorphs

| | Occurrences | | Sites |
	No.	%	No.
Trapezoidal torso	5	11	2
Triangular torso	17	40	9
Basal element	5	11	2
Horns	12	28	8
Plumes	1	2	1
Facial features	2	5	2
Earbobs	1	2	1
Dominance	3	7	2

Table 5. (continued)

C. Quadrupeds

| | Occurrences | | Sites |
	No.	%	No.
Mountain sheep	68	61	12
Deer	5	4	3
Other or unidentified	39	35	14
Total	112	100	19

D. Abstract Elements

| | Occurrences | | Sites |
	No.	%	No.
Pottery or textile type of design	4	2	4
Rectilinear spiral	1	1/2	1
Zigzag, single or double	6	3	5
Wavy lines, single or double	21	10	9
One-pole ladder	2	1	2
Dots or dot design	15	7	6
Circle	7	3	3
Wandering line	9	4	5
Straight line	6	3	5
Connected circles	3	1	1
Rake	8	4	4
Sawtooth	8	4	6
Sun disc	1	1/2	1
Sectioned circle	1	1/2	1
Spoked circle	1	1/2	1
Bisected circle	1	1/2	1
Nest of chevrons	1	1/2	1
Spiral	18	9	7
Concentric circles	7	3	6
Two-pole ladder	2	1	2
Unidentified	89	42	16
Total	211	100	23

Twenty-four of the panels in Table 5 are carved and 5 are painted.

Table 6.   Elements at 77 Sites of the Great Basin Curvilinear Style, with a Representational Component, in Western Utah

A.   Major Element Categories

		Occurrences		Sites
		No.	%	No.
Anthropomorph:	solid	8		8
	stick	28		21
	Total	36	5	27
Quadruped:	solid	29		18
	stick	45		23
	Total (including 56 mountain sheep)	74	11	37
Other representational:				
	hand- or footprint	3		2
	serpent	3		3
	Total	6	1	5
All representational elements		116	17	51
Abstract elements		549	83	72
Total all elements		665	100	77

B.   Abstract Elements

	Occurrences		Sites
	No.	%	No.
Circle	30	6	20
Concentric circle or semicircle	13	2	11
Bisected circle	45	8	28
Sectioned circle	5	1	4
Spoked concentric circle	2	t	2
Tailed circle	48	9	26

Table 6. (continued)

B.   Abstract Elements (continued)

| | Occurrences | | Sites |
	No.	%	No.
Circle with dot	3	t	3
Circle cluster	2	t	2
Connected circles	21	4	12
Chain of circles	8	1	4
Sun disc	6	1	6
Spiral	2	t	2
Curvilinear meander	80	15	32
Dots or dot design	3	t	3
Wavy lines	20	4	12
Deer hoof	4	t	4
Rectilinear meander	6	1	5
Rectangular	5	1	6
Cross	30	6	15
Parallel straight lines	10	2	4
Sawtooth	2	t	2
Zigzag line	10	2	7
One-pole ladder	27	5	17
Two-pole ladder	1	t	1
Rake	18	3	11
Cross-hatching	1	t	1
Triangle	4	t	4
Straight line	25	5	14
Convoluted rake	1	t	1
Row of short lines	3	t	2
Bird track	8	1	5
Abstract face or mask	2	t	2
Miscellaneous	103	19	34
Total	549	100	72

The presence of representational figures tabulated in association with sites in Table 6 is explained in the text. The element list with certain modifications is that of Heizer and Baumhoff (1962, Table 2, p. 73). In the current study the triangle occurring alone was distinguished from a series of triangles attached to a base line. The latter is classified throughout this study as a sawtooth element. Added to Heizer and Baumhoff's list are the straight line, the row of short lines, and the abstract face or mask. The plant form, bird track, and deer hoof are classified here, as in Heizer and Baumhoff, as abstract elements since their representational significance is questionable.

Table 7.   A Comparison between Barrier Canyon Style and Fremont Work.

	Barrier Canyon	Fremont
LARGE ANTHROPOMORPHS torso form	Usually extremely elongate, tapering or rectangular. Rarely broadly trapezoidal or triangular.	Trapezoidal or triangular without excessive elongation. Waist constriction and kilt flare common.
head form	May be large and round, rectangular, or bucket-shaped. Also often small, rounded, insignificant. Sometimes absent.	Always large, round, rectangular, or bucket-shaped.
headdress	Simple, usually delicate. Occurring regularly are rabbit-ear-like projections, thin, short antennae, long antennae, crown of dots or short thin lines. Horns as such rare.	Helmet, inverted bucket, antlers, horns. Horns most common; may be fringed. Plumes, feathers, infinite variety of elaborations in Classic Vernal Style. Occasional rabbit-eared figures in southern San Rafael.
earrings	Thin lines.	Round earbobs.
facial decoration	Features usually absent. Round oversized eyes, like death's head, occasional. Bug-eyed figures. Some painted white dot or linear abstract designs.	Masks or facial features (eyes and mouth) commonly depicted. Slit eyes in south. Weeping-eye motif and occasional further elaboration. Abstract design only in Conger.
neck decoration	Occasional. Vertical stripes.	Occasional. Dots or horizontal stripes.
torso decoration	Horizontal bands with textilelike designs; inset panel with stripes or dotted lines; vertical striping or vertical wavy lines, or center vertical panel stripe.	Torso commonly divided by sash at waist. Kilt may be indicated. Necklace very common, beaded or yoke type. Vertical center line may occur between necklace and waist. Diagonal line crosses torso in southern San Rafael. Heavy stripes.
arms and hands	Often lacking. Arms usually short. May be held out straight or raised. If present, often hold something.	Usually present or at least suggested, except in number of southern San Rafael sites. Normally held down. Long. May be jointed at elbow so lower arm and hand upraised. Splayed fingers common.
objects held in hands	Wild grasses, other plants, possible gathering tools and snakes. Shields at one site.	Commonly hold shields, heads, rakes, staffs, and implements.
flanking figures	Wavy lines, circle motifs and zoomorphs (see below).	None.
OTHER LIFE FORMS	Relatively few in number. Tiny birds and animals (mountain sheep and others) near shoulders, in headgear, flanking, or arranged in composition around large anthropomorphs. Also large and small quadrupeds resembling dogs may accompany large anthropomorph.	Small anthropomorphs, including hunters, occur in large numbers usually. Quadrupeds (mountain sheep, deer, elk, and bison) found at random without relationship to large anthropomorphic figures. Snakes in San Rafael sites. Birds rare.
ABSTRACT ELEMENTS	Very rare.	Prolific. Large inventory of abstract designs with wavy line, spiral, concentric circle, and dot designs among most popular.

Table 8. Table listing the Abstract Elements Present in Nevada Sites (after Heizer and Baumhoff, 1962, p. 173, Table 3) and Showing Their Occurrence in Utah Fremont Sites.

Abstract Elements in Nevada Sites	Ashley-Dry Fork Valleys	Dinosaur Nat'l Mon.	N. San Rafael Zone	Clear Creek Canyon
1. circle	X	X	X	X
2. concentric circle	X	X	X	X
3. bisected circle				X
4. sectioned circle				X
5. spoked or spoked concentric circle	X		X	X
6. tailed circle				
7. circle and dot	X		X	
8. circle cluster	X		X	
9. connected circles			X	X
10. chain of circles			X	
11. sun disc	X	X	X	X
12. spiral	X	X	X	X
13. curvilinear meander (wandering line)	X		X	X
14. convoluted rake				
15. connected dots				
16. dumbbell				
17. dot or dot design	X	X	X	X
18. wavy lines	X	X	X	X
19. deer hoof				
20. oval grid				
21. rectangular grid				
22. blocked oval				
23. cross or star	X		X	
24. bird tracks				
25. parallel straight lines				
26. triangle (sawtooth)	X		X	X
27. lozenge chain			X	
28. zigzag	X		X	X
29. ladder (one-pole)	X	X	X	X
30. ladder (two-pole)				X
31. rake	X		X	X
32. rain symbol				
33. rectilinear meander	X			
34. chevrons				X
35. radiating dashes				
36. crosshatch				
37. plant form	X			
TOTAL NUMBER	17	7	18	17
PERCENTAGE OF 37	46	19	49	46

Bibliography

Adams, William Y. and Nettie K. Adams
   1959. *An Inventory of Prehistoric Sites on the Lower San Juan River, Utah.* Museum of Northern Arizona, Bulletin 31 (Glen Canyon Series no. 1), Flagstaff.

Adams, William Y., Alexander J. Lindsay, Jr. and Christy G. Turner, II
   1961. *Survey and Excavations in Lower Glen Canyon, 1952–1958.* Museum of Northern Arizona, Bulletin 36 (Glen Canyon Series, no. 3), Flagstaff.

Adovasio, J. M.
   1986. Prehistoric Basketry. In *Great Basin*, edited by Warren L. D'Azevedo, 194–205. Handbook of North American Indians, vol. 11, William C. Sturtevant, general editor. Smithsonian Institution, Washington.

Aikens, C. Melvin
   1965. *Excavations in Southwest Utah.* University of Utah Anthropological Papers, no. 76 (Glen Canyon Series, no. 27).
   1966a. *Virgin-Kayenta Cultural Relationships.* University of Utah Anthropological Papers, no. 79.
   1966b. *Fremont-Promontory-Plains Relationships.* University of Utah Anthropological Papers, no. 82.
   1967a. *Excavations at Snake Rock Village and the Bear River No. 2 Site.* University of Utah Anthropological Papers, no. 87.
   1967b. "Plains Relationships of the Fremont Culture: A Hypothesis," *American Antiquity*, vol. 32, no. 2, pp. 198–209.
   1970. "Whence and Whither the Fremont Culture, a Restatement of the Problem." Paper prepared for the Fremont Culture Symposium, 35th Annual Meeting of the Society of American Archaeology, Mexico City.

Allen, Mary K.
   1992. New Frontiers in Rock Art: The Grand Canyon. *American Indian Rock Art* 15:49–70, edited by Kay K. Sanger. San Miguel, California.

Ambler, John Richard
   1966a. *Caldwell Village and Fremont Prehistory.* Doctoral Dissertation, (University Microfilms 67–9961), University of Colorado, Boulder.
   1966b. *Caldwell Village.* University of Utah Anthropological Papers, no. 84.
   1969. "The Temporal Span of the Fremont," *Southwestern Lore*, vol. 34, no. 4, pp. 107–117.
   1970. "Just What Is Fremont?" Paper prepared for the Fremont Culture Symposium, 35th Annual Meeting of the Society for American Archaeology, Mexico City.

Anderson, Keith M.
   1963. "Ceramic Clues to Pueblo-Puebloid Relationships," *American Antiquity*, vol. 28, no. 3, pp. 303–307.

Baldwin, Gordon C.
   1947. "An Archaeological Reconnaissance of the Yampa and Green Rivers," *The Kiva*, vol. 12, no. 3, pp. 31–36, Tucson.
   1949. "Archaeological Survey in Southeastern Utah," *Southwestern Journal of Anthropology*, vol. 5, pp. 393–404.

Bannister, Bryant, Jeffrey S. Dean and William J. Robinson
   1969. *Tree-Ring Dates from Utah S–W, Southern Utah Area.* Laboratory of Tree-Ring Research, University of Arizona, Tucson.

Bard, J. C., F. Asaro and R. F. Heizer
   1978. Perspectives on the Dating of Prehistoric Great Basin Petroglyphs by Neutron Activation Analysis. *Archaeometry* 20:85–88.

Beauvais, Lester
   1955. "Primitive People of the Gunnison Basin," *Southwestern Lore*, vol. 21, no. 3, pp. 29–34.

Beckwith, Frank
   1931. "Some Interesting Pictographs in Nine Mile Canyon, Utah," *El Palacio*, vol. 31, no. 14, pp. 216–222, Santa Fe.
   1934. "A Group of Petroglyphs near Moab, Utah," *El Palacio*, vol. 36, nos. 23–24, pp. 177–178, Santa Fe.

Birney, Hoffman
   1933. "Archaeological Sites in Glen Canyon of the Colorado: a Preliminary Report." Unpublished manuscript, Peabody Museum, Harvard University.

Breternitz, David A.
   1970. "The Eastern Uinta Fremont." Paper prepared for the Fremont Culture Symposium, 35th Annual Meeting of the Society for American Archaeology, Mexico City.

Buckles, William Gayl
   1964. "An Analysis of Primitive Rock Art at Medicine Creek Cave, Wyoming, and its Cultural and Chronological Relationships to the Prehistory of the Plains." Master's thesis, University of Colorado, Boulder.
   1965. "An Appraisal of Fremont Culture-Shoshonean Relationships," *Plains Anthropologist*, vol. 10, no. 27, pp. 54–55.

Burgh, Robert F.
   1950. "A Fremont Basket Maker House in Dinosaur National Monument," *Tree-Ring Bulletin*, vol. 16, no. 3, pp. 19–20, Tucson.

Burgh, Robert F. and Charles R. Scoggin
   1948. *The Archaeology of Castle Park, Dinosaur National Monument.* University of Colorado Studies, Series in Anthropology, no. 2.

Burton, Robert Jordan
  1971. The Pictographs and Petroglyphs of Dinosaur National Monument. M.A. thesis, Department of Anthropology, University of Colorado, Boulder.

Carter, George F.
  1945. *Plant Geography and Culture History in the American Southwest.* Viking Fund Publication in Anthropology, no. 5, New York.

Castleton, Kenneth B.
  1978. *Petroglyphs and Pictographs of Utah.* Vol. 1. *The East and Northeast.* Utah Museum of Natural History, Salt Lake City.
  1979. *Petroglyphs and Pictographs of Utah.* Vol. 2. *The South, Central, West, and Northwest.* Utah Museum of Natural History, Salt Lake City.

Castleton, Kenneth B. and David B. Madsen
  1981. The Distribution of Rock Art Elements and Style in Utah. *Journal of California and Great Basin Anthropology* 3 (2):163–175.

Cole, Sally J.
  1984. Analysis of a San Juan (Basketmaker) Style Painted Mask in Grand Gulch, Utah, *Southwestern Lore* 50 (1):1–6.
  1985. Additional Information on Basketmaker Masks or Faces in Southeastern Utah. *Southwestern Lore* 51 (1):14–18.
  1989. Iconography and Symbolism in Basketmaker Rock Art. In "Rock Art in the Western Canyons." Jane S. Day, Paul D. Friedman, and Marcia J. Tate, eds., 59–85. *Colorado Archaeological Society Memoir* 3, Denver Museum of Natural History.
  1990. *Legacy on Stone: The Rock Art of the Colorado Plateau and the Four Corners Area.* Johnson Books, Boulder.

Colton, Harold S.
  1952. *Pottery Types of the Arizona Strip and Adjacent Areas in Utah and Nevada.* Museum of Northern Arizona, Ceramic Series, no. 1, Flagstaff.

Conner, Stuart W.
  1962. "The Fish Creek, Owl Canyon and Grinnvoll Rock Shelter Pictograph Sites in Montana," *Plains Anthropologist,* vol. 7, no. 15, pp. 24–35.

Coulam, Nancy J.
  1992. Radiocarbon Dating of the All American Man. *Canyon Legacy* 16:28–29.

Crane, H. R. and J. B. Griffin
  1958. "University of Michigan Radiocarbon Dates III," *Science,* vol. 128, pp. 1117–1123.
  1959. "University of Michigan Radiocarbon Dates IV," *American Journal of Science,* Radiocarbon Supplement, vol. 1, pp. 173–198.

Cutler, Hugh C.
  1966a. "Maize from Caldwell Village," in Ambler *Caldwell Village and Fremont Prehistory,* (University Microfilms 67–9961) University of Colorado, Boulder.
  1966b. *Corn, Cucurbits and Cotton from Glen Canyon.* University of Utah Anthropological Papers, no. 80.

Day, Kent C. and David S. Dibble
  1963. *Archaeological Survey of the Flaming Gorge Reservoir Area, Wyoming, Utah.* University of Utah Anthropological Papers, no. 65 (Upper Colorado Series, no. 9).

Dellenbaugh, F. S.
  1877. "The Shinumos—A Pre-Historic People of the Rocky Mountain Region," *Bulletin of the Buffalo Society of Natural Sciences,* vol. 3, no. 4.

Euler, Robert C.
  1964. "Southern Paiute Archaeology," *American Antiquity,* vol. 29, no. 3, pp. 379–381.

Ferguson, C. W., Jr.
  1949. "Additional Dates for Nine Mile Canyon, Northeastern Utah," *Tree-Ring Bulletin,* vol. 16, no. 2, pp. 10–11, Tucson.

Flaim, Francis and Austen D. Warburton
  1961. "Additional Figurines from Rasmussen Cave," *The Masterkey,* vol. 35, no. 1, pp. 19–24.

Foster, Gene
  1954. "Petrographic Art in Glen Canyon," *Plateau,* vol. 27, no. 1, pp. 6–18, Flagstaff.

Fowler, Catherine S. and Don D. Fowler
  1981. The Southern Paiute: A.D. 1400–1776. In *The Protohistoric Period in the North American Southwest, A.D. 1450–1700,* David R. Wilcox and W. Bruce Masse, editors, pp. 129–62. Arizona State University, Anthropological Research Papers no. 24. Tempe.

Fowler, Don D.
  1959a. *The Glen Canyon Main Stem Survey.* University of Utah Anthropological Papers, no. 39 (Glen Canyon Series, no. 6), pp. 473–539.
  1959b. *The Glen Canyon Archeological Survey.* University of Utah Anthropological Papers, no. 39. (Glen Canyon Series, no. 6), pp. 1–93.
  1963. *1961 Excavations, Harris Wash, Utah.* University of Utah Anthropological Papers, no. 64.
  1970. "The Western Fremont." Paper prepared for the Fremont Culture Symposium, 35th Annual Meeting of the Society for American Archaeology, Mexico City.

Fowler, Don D. and C. Melvin Aikens
  1963. *1961 Excavations, Kaiparowits Plateau, Utah.* University of Utah Anthropological Papers, no. 66 (Glen Canyon Series, no. 20).

Fry, Gary
  1970. "Salt Lake Fremont." Paper prepared for the Fremont Culture Symposium, 35th Annual Meeting of the Society for American Archaeology, Mexico City.

Gaumer, Alfred Elliott
  1937. "Basketmaker Caves in Desolation Cañon, Green River, Utah," *The Masterkey,* vol. 11, no. 5, pp. 160–165.

Gebhard, David
  1958. "19 Centuries of American Abstraction," *Art News,* vol. 56, no. 10, pp. 20–23.

1960. *Prehistoric Paintings of the Diablo Region—a Preliminary Report*. Publications in Art and Science, no. 3, Roswell Museum and Art Center, Roswell, New Mexico.
1966. "The Shield Motif in Plains Rock Art," *American Antiquity*, vol. 31, no. 5, part 1, pp. 721–732.

Gebhard, David S. and Harold A. Cahn
1950. "The Petroglyphs of Dinwoody, Wyoming," *American Antiquity*, vol. 15, no. 3, pp. 219–228.

Gieb, Phil R. and Helen C. Fairley
1992. Radiocarbon Dating of Fremont Anthropomorphic Rock Art in Glen Canyon, South-central Utah. *Journal of Field Archaeology* 19(2). Boston University.

Gifford, E. W.
1940. "Cultural Element Distributions: XII, Apache-Pueblo," University of California Anthropological Records, vol. 4, no. 1, Berkeley and Los Angeles.

Gillin, John
1938. "Archaeological Investigations in Nine Mile Canyon, Utah," *Bulletin of the University of Utah*, vol. 28, no. 11.

Gladwin, Winifred and Harold S. Gladwin
1934. *A Method for Designation of Cultures and their Variations*. Medallion Papers, no. 15, Gila Pueblo, Globe.

Grant, Campbell
1967. *Rock Art of the American Indian*. Thomas Y. Crowell Co., New York.

Grant, Campbell, James W. Baird and J. Kenneth Pringle
1968. *Rock Drawings of the Coso Range*. Maturango Museum, Publication no. 4, China Lake.

Greenwood, Geraldine M.
1956. *Petroglyphs of the Parowan Valley and Vicinity*. University of Utah Anthropological Papers, no. 25, pp. 109–118.

Guernsey, Samuel J.
1931. *Explorations in Northeastern Arizona*. Papers of the Peabody Museum, Harvard University, vol. 12, no. 1.

Gunnerson, James H.
1956. "A Fluted Point Site in Utah," *American Antiquity*, vol. 21, no. 4, pp. 412–414.
1957. *An Archeological Survey of the Fremont Area*. University of Utah Anthropological Papers, no. 28.
1959a. *Archeological Survey of the Kaiparowits Plateau*. University of Utah Anthropological Papers, no. 39 (Glen Canyon Series, no. 6), pp. 319–469.
1959b. *1957 Excavations, Glen Canyon Area*. University of Utah Anthropological Papers, no. 43 (Glen Canyon Series, no. 10).
1960. "The Fremont Culture: Internal Dimensions and External Relationships," *American Antiquity*, vol. 25, no. 3, pp. 373–380.
1962. "Plateau Shoshonean Prehistory: A Suggested Reconstruction," *American Antiquity*, vol. 28, no. 1, pp. 41–45.
1969. *The Fremont Culture: A Study in Culture Dynamics on the Northern Anasazi Frontier*. Papers of

the Peabody Museum, Harvard University, vol. 59, no. 2.

Harrington, E. P.
1933. "More Kachina Pictographs in Nevada," *The Masterkey*, vol. 7, no. 2, pp. 48–50.

Harrington, M. R.
1932. "The Kachina Rockshelter in Nevada," *The Masterkey*, vol. 6, no. 5, pp. 148–151.
1934. "American Horses and Ancient Men in Nevada," *The Masterkey*, vol. 8, pp. 164–169.
1944. "Prehistoric Dots and Dashes," *The Masterkey*, vol. 18, no. 6, p. 196.

Haury, Emil
1945. *Painted Cave, Northeastern Arizona*. The Amerind Foundation, Inc., Publications, no. 3.

Hedges, Ken
1985. Rock Art Portrayals of Shamanic Transformation and Magical Flight. *Rock Art Papers* 2 (*San Diego Museum Papers* 18), Ken Hedges, editor, pp. 83–94. Museum of Man, San Diego.

Heizer, Robert F. and Martin A. Baumhoff
1962. *Prehistoric Rock Art of Nevada and Eastern California*. University of California Press, Berkeley and Los Angeles.

Henderson, Randall
1949. "19 Days on Utah Trails," *Desert Magazine*, vol. 12, pp. 5–11, and vol. 13, pp. 19–25.

Hogan, P. F., L. Losee and J. Dodge
1975. Archaeological Investigations in the Maze District, Canyonlands National Park, Utah. Department of Anthropology, University of Utah, Salt Lake City. Submitted to National Park Service, Rocky Mountain Regional Office, Denver.

Hull, Frank W. and Nancy M. White
1980. Spindle Whorls, Incised and Painted Stone, and Unfired Clay Objects. In "Cowboy Cave," Jesse D. Jennings, ed., pp. 117–127. *University of Utah Anthropological Papers*, 104, Salt Lake City.

Hunt, Alice P.
1953. *Archeological Survey of the La Sal Mountain Area, Utah*. University of Utah Anthropological Papers, no. 14.

Hurst, Winston and Bruce D. Louthan
1979. Survey of Rock Art in the Central Portion of Nine Mile Canyon Eastern Utah. *Publications in Archaeology*, Department of Anthropology and Archaeology, Brigham Young University, New Series, no. 4, Salt Lake City.

Jameson, Sydney
1958. *Archaeological Notes on Stansbury Island*. University of Utah Anthropological Papers, no. 34.

Jennings, Jesse D. (editor)
1956. "The American Southwest: A Problem in Cultural Isolation," in *Seminars in Archaeology: 1955*, edited by Robert Wauchope, Memoirs of the Society for American Archaeology, no. 11, pp. 61–127, Salt Lake City.
1957. *Danger Cave*. University of Utah Anthropological Papers, no. 27.

Jennings, Jesse D. and Edward Norbeck
1955. "Great Basin Prehistory: A Review," *American Antiquity,* vol. 21, no. 1, pp. 1–11.

Jennings, Jesse D. and Floyd Sharrock
1965. "The Glen Canyon: A Multi-Disciplines Project," *Utah Historical Quarterly,* vol. 33, no. 1, pp. 34–50.

Jones, Carl H.
1961. "An Archaeological Survey of Utah County, Utah." Master's thesis, Brigham Young University.

Judd, Neil M.
1926. *Archeological Observations North of the Rio Colorado.* Bureau of American Ethnology, Bulletin 82, Washington, D.C.
1930. *The Excavation and Repair of Betatakin.* Proceedings of the United States National Museum, vol. 77, art. 5, Publication no. 2828. Washington, D.C.

Kelley, Charles
1943. "We Found a Gallery of Indian Etchings," *Desert Magazine,* vol. 6, no. 11, pp. 18–19.

Kidder, A. V. and Samuel Guernsey
1919. *Explorations in Northeastern Arizona.* Bureau of American Ethnology, Bulletin 65, Washington, D.C.

Lipe, William D.
1960. *1958 Excavations, Glen Canyon Area.* University of Utah Anthropological Papers, no. 44 (Glen Canyon Series, no. 11).

Lister, Florence C.
1964. *Kaiparowits Plateau and Glen Canyon Prehistory: An Interpretation Based on Ceramics.* University of Utah Anthropological Papers, no. 71 (Glen Canyon Series, no. 23).

Lister, Robert H.
1951. *Excavations at Hells Midden, Dinosaur National Monument.* University of Colorado, Series in Anthropology, no. 3, Boulder.
1958. *The Glen Canyon Survey in 1957.* University of Utah Anthropological Papers, no. 30 (Glen Canyon Series, no. 1).
1959a. *The Glen Canyon Right Bank Survey.* University of Utah Anthropological Papers, no. 39 (Glen Canyon Series, no. 6), pp. 27–161.
1959b. *The Waterpocket Fold: A Distributional Problem.* University of Utah Anthropological Papers, no. 39, (Glen Canyon Series, no. 6), pp. 285–317.

Lister, Robert H. and Herbert W. Dick
1952. "Archaeology of the Glade Park Area—A Progress Report," *Southwestern Lore,* vol. 17, no. 4, pp. 69–92.

Lister, Robert H. and Florence C. Lister
1961. *The Coombs Site, Part III, Summary and Conclusions.* University of Utah Anthropological Papers, no. 41 (Glen Canyon Series, no. 8).

McGregor, John C.
1965. *Southwestern Archaeology.* 2nd ed., University of Illinois Press, Urbana.

Madsen, David B.
1986. Prehistoric Ceramics. In *Great Basin,* edited by Warren L. D'Azevedo, pp. 206–214. Handbook of North American Indians, vol. 11, William C. Sturtevant, general editor. Smithsonian Institution, Washington, D.C.

Mallery, Garrick
1886. "Pictographs of the North American Indians: A Preliminary Paper," Bureau of American Ethnology, *4th Annual Report,* 1882–83.
1893. "Picture-Writing of the American Indians," Bureau of American Ethnology, *10th Annual Report,* 1888–1889.

Malouf, Carling
1941. "Notes on the Archeology of the Barrier Cañon Region, Utah," *The Masterkey,* vol. 15, no. 4, pp. 150–153.
1946. "The Deep Creek Region, the Northwestern Frontier of the Pueblo Culture," *American Antiquity,* vol. 12, no. 2, pp. 117–121.

Marwitt, John P.
1970. "Parowan Fremont." Paper prepared for the Fremont Culture Symposium, 35th Annual Meeting of the Society for American Archaeology, Mexico City.

Meighan, Clement W. and Norman E. Coles, Frank D. Davis, Geraldine M. Greenwood, William M. Harrison and E. Heath MacBain.
1956. *Archeological Excavations in Iron County, Utah.* University of Utah Anthropological Papers, no. 25.

Morss, Noel
1931. *The Ancient Culture of the Fremont River in Utah.* Papers of the Peabody Museum, Harvard University, vol. 12, no. 3.
1954. *Clay Figurines of the American Southwest.* Papers of the Peabody Museum, Harvard University, vol. 49, no. 1.

Mulloy, William
1952. "A Preliminary Historical Outline for the Northwestern Plains." Dissertation submitted to Faculty of Division of the Social Sciences, University of Chicago.
1954. *Archaeological Investigations in the Shoshone Basin of Wyoming.* University of Wyoming Publications, vol. 18, no. 1, pp. 1–70.
1958. *A Preliminary Historical Outline for the Northwestern Plains.* University of Wyoming Publications, vol. 22, no. 1.

Murbarger, Nell
1960. "First Pack Train Over the Tavaputs," *Desert Magazine,* vol. 23, no. 3, pp. 24–27 and 34.

Newcomb, W. W., Jr.
1967. *The Rock Art of Texas Indians.* Paintings by Forrest Kirkland. University of Texas Press, Austin and London.

Noxon, John and Deborah Marcus
1982. Significant Rock Art Sites in Arches and Canyonlands National Parks and in Natural Bridges National Monument, Southeastern Utah. Submitted to USDI National Park Service, Purchase Order

nos. PX 1340–9–A434 and PX 1340–0–A338. Copies available from Canyonlands National Park, Moab.

1985. *Significant Rock Art Sites in the Needles District of Canyonlands National Park, Southeastern Utah.* Submitted to USDI National Park Service, Purchase Order nos. PX 1340–2–A099 and PX 1340–3–A334. Copies available from Canyonlands National Park, Moab.

Nusbaum, Jesse L.
1922. *A Basket-Maker Cave in Kane County, Utah: with Notes on the Artifacts by A. V. Kidder and S. J. Guernsey.* Indian Notes and Monographs, Heye Foundation, no. 29, New York.

Pierson, Lloyd
1962. "Archaeological Resources of the Needles–Salt Creek Area, Utah," *Utah Archaeology,* vol. 8, no. 2, pp. 1–3.

Putnam, J. D.
1876. "Hieroglyphics Observed in Summit Cañon, Utah and on Little Popo-agie River in Wyoming," *Proceedings of the Davenport Academy of Natural Sciences,* 1867–1876, Vol. 1, pp. 143–145.

Reagan, Albert B.
1917. "The Deep Creek Indians," *El Palacio,* vol. 4, no. 3, pp. 30–42.
1931a. "Some Archaeological Notes on Nine Mile Canyon, Utah," *El Palacio,* vol. 31, no. 4, pp. 45–71.
1931b. "Additional Archaeological Notes on Ashley and Dry Fork Canyons in Northeastern Utah," *El Palacio,* vol. 31, no. 8, pp. 122–131.
1931c. "Some Archaeological Notes on Hill Canyon in Northeastern Utah," *El Palacio,* vol. 31, no. 15, pp. 223-244.
1931d. "Ruins and Pictographs in Nine Mile Canyon, Utah," *Transactions of the Illinois State Academy of Science,* vol. 24, no. 2, pp. 369–370.
1932. "Some Notes on the Picture Writing North of Mexico," *Bulletin of the Wagner Free Institute of Science of Philadelphia,* vol. 7, no. 4.
1933a. "Anciently Inhabited Caves of the Vernal (Utah) District, with some Additional Notes on Nine Mile Canyon, Northeast Utah," *Transactions of the Kansas Academy of Science,* vol. 36, pp. 41–70.
1933b. "Indian Pictures in Ashley and Dry Fork Valleys in Northeastern Utah," *Art and Archaeology,* vol. 34, no. 4, pp. 201–210.
1934. "The Gosiute (Goshute) or Shoshoni-Goship Indians of the Deep Creek Region in Western Utah," *Utah Academy of Sciences, Art and Letters,* vol. 11, pp. 43–54.
1935. "Petroglyphs Show that the Ancients of the Southwest Wore Masks," *American Anthropologist,* vol. 37, no. 4, pp. 707–708.
n.d. "Some Notes on the Archaeology of Ashley and Dry Fork Valleys in Northeastern Utah." Manuscript, Museum of New Mexico, Santa Fe.

Roberts, Frank H. H., Jr.
1929. *Shabik'eshchee Village: A Late Basket Maker Site in Chaco Canyon, New Mexico.* Bureau of American Ethnology, Bulletin 92, Washington, D.C.

Rudy, Jack R.
1953. *Archeological Survey of Western Utah.* University of Utah Anthropological Papers, no. 12.
1954. *Pine Park Shelter, Washington County, Utah.* University of Utah Anthropological Papers, no. 18.
1955. *Archeological Excavations in Beef Basin, Utah.* University of Utah Anthropological Papers, no. 20.

Rudy, Jack R. and Robert D. Stirland
1950. *An Archeological Reconnaisance in Washington County, Utah.* University of Utah Anthropological Papers, no. 9.

Russ, J. M. Hyman, H. J. Shafer, and M. W. Rowe
1990. Radiocarbon Dating of Prehistoric Rock Paintings by Selective Oxidation of Organic Carbon. *Nature* 348:710–711.

Schaafsma, Polly
1963. *Rock Art in the Navajo Reservoir District.* Papers in Anthropology, no. 7, Museum of New Mexico, Santa Fe.
1966a. *Early Navaho Rock Paintings and Carvings.* Museum of Navaho Ceremonial Art, Santa Fe.
1966b. "A Survey of Tsegi Canyon Rock Art." Manuscript, National Park Service files, Santa Fe.
1968. "The Los Lunas Petroglyphs," *El Palacio,* vol. 75, no. 2.
1970. Survey report of the rock art of Utah. Ms. on file, University of Utah Archeological Laboratory.
1980. *Indian Rock Art of the Southwest.* School of American Research and University of New Mexico Press, Santa Fe and Albuquerque.
1986. Rock Art. In *Great Basin,* pp. 215–226. Handbook of North American Indians 11, William C. Sturtevant, general editor, Warren L. D'Azevedo, volume editor. Smithsonian Institution, Washington, D.C.
1990. Shaman's Gallery: A Grand Canyon Rock Art Site. *Kiva* 55 (3):213–234. Arizona Archaeological and Historical Society, Tucson.
1992. Imagery and Magic: Petroglyphs at Comanche Gap, Galisteo Basin, New Mexico. In "Archaeology, Art, and Anthropology," edited by Meliha S. Duran and David T. Kirkpatrick, *The Archaeological Society of New Mexico*: 18:157–174, Albuquerque.

Schapiro, Meyer
1953. "Style," in *Anthropology Today,* A. L. Kroeber, ed., University of Chicago Press, pp. 287–312.

Schroeder, Albert H.
1953. "A Few Sites in Moapa Valley, Nevada," *The Masterkey,* vol. 27, no. 2.
1955. *Archeology of Zion Park.* University of Utah Anthropological Papers, no. 22.
1963. "Comments on Gunnerson's Plateau Shoshonean Prehistory," *American Antiquity,* vol. 28, no. 4, pp. 559–560.

Schulman, Edmund
1948. "Dendrochronology in Northeastern Utah," *Tree-Ring Bulletin,* vol. 15, no. 1/2, Tucson.
1950. "A Dated Beam from Dinosaur National Monument," *Tree-Ring Bulletin,* vol. 16, no. 3, pp. 18–19, Tucson.

1951. "Miscellaneous Ring Records," *Tree-Ring Bulletin,* vol. 17, no. 4, pp. 28–30, Tucson.

Sharrock, Floyd W.
1966a. *Prehistoric Occupation Patterns in Southwest Wyoming and Cultural Relationships with the Great Basin and Plains Culture areas.* University of Utah Anthropological Papers, no. 77.
1966b. *An Archeological Survey of Canyonlands National Park.* University of Utah Anthropological Papers, no. 83, pp. 49–84.

Sharrock, Floyd W. and John P. Marwitt
1967. *Excavations at Nephi, Utah, 1965–1966.* University of Utah Anthropological Papers, no 88.

Shields, Wayne F.
1970. "The Fremont Culture in the Uinta Basin." Paper prepared for the Fremont Culture Symposium, 35th Annual Meeting of the Society for American Archaeology, Mexico City.

Shutler, Richard, Jr.
1961. *Lost City: Pueblo Grande de Nevada.* Nevada State Museum, Anthropological Papers, no. 5, Carson City.

Shutler, Richard, Jr., and Mary Elizabeth Shutler
1962. *Archeological Survey in Southern Nevada.* Nevada State Museum, Anthropological Papers, no. 7, Carson City.

Sleight, Frederick W.
1946. "Comments on Basketmaker-Like Pictographs in Northern Utah," *The Masterkey,* vol. 20, no. 3, pp. 88–92.

Steward, Julian H.
1929. *Petroglyphs of California and Adjoining States.* University of California Publications in American Archeology and Ethnology, vol. 24, pp. 47–238.
1933a. *Archaeological Problems of the Northern Periphery of the Southwest.* Museum of Northern Arizona, Bulletin 5, Flagstaff.
1933b. "The Archaeology of Glen Canyon of the Colorado River." Manuscript, Peabody Museum, Harvard University.
1936. *Pueblo Material Culture in Western Utah.* University of New Mexico Bulletin, Anthropological Series, vol. 1, no. 3.
1937a. *Ancient Caves of the Great Salt Lake Region.* Bureau of American Ethnology, Bulletin 116.
1937b. "Petroglyphs of the United States," *Smithsonian Report for 1936,* pp. 405–425.
1941. *Archeological Reconnaissance of Southern Utah.* Bureau of American Ethnology, Bulletin, no. 128, pp. 277–356.

Suhm, Dee Ann
1959. *Extended Survey of the Right Bank of the Glen Canyon.* University of Utah Anthropological Papers, no. 39 (Glen Canyon Series, no. 6), pp. 163–285.

Taylor, Dee C.
1957. *Two Fremont Sites and Their Position in Southwestern Prehistory.* University of Utah Anthropological Papers, no. 29.

Tipps, Betsy L. and Nancy J. Hewitt
1989. Cultural Resource Inventory and Testing in the Salt Creek Pocket and Devils Lane Areas, Needles District, Canyonlands National Park, Utah. *Selections from the Division of Cultural Resources,* no. 1, Rocky Mountain Region, National Park Service, Denver.

Turner, Christy G., II
1963. *Petroglyphs of the Glen Canyon Region.* Museum of Northern Arizona, Bulletin 38 (Glen Canyon Series, no. 4), Flagstaff.
1971. Revised Dating for Early Rock Art of the Glen Canyon Region. *American Antiquity* 36:469–471.

Utah Archaeology
1964. Cover illustration, vol. 19, no. 2.

Vogel, Beatrice R.
1952. "Baker Creek Pictograph Cave," *Monthly Report of the Stanford Grotto,* National Speleological Society, vol. 2, pp. 107–108.

Wauer, Roland
1965. *Pictograph Site in Cave Valley, Zion National Park, Utah.* University of Utah Anthropological Papers, no. 75 (Miscellaneous Papers, no. 9), pp. 57–84.

Whitley, David S. and Ronald I. Dorn
1988. Cation–Ratio Dating of Petroglyphs Using PIXE. *Nuclear Instruments and Methods in Physics Research* B35:410–414. Amsterdam.

Wormington, H. M.
1951. *Prehistoric Indians of the Southwest.* The Denver Museum of Natural History, Popular Series no. 7, 2nd ed., Denver.
1955. *A Reappraisal of the Fremont Culture.* Proceedings of the Denver Museum of Natural History, no. 1.

Wormington, H. M. and R. H. Lister
1956. *Archaeological Investigations on the Uncompahgre Plateau in West Central Colorado.* Proceedings of the Denver Museum of Natural History, no. 2.

Young, Levi E.
1929. "The Ancient Inhabitants of Utah," *Art and Archaeology,* vol. 27, no. 3, pp. 124–135.